The Original
SINGAPORE SLING
Book

FAN SEE!
OVERHEARD AT RAFFLES.

She to He: "We must be dancing awfully well, darling.
Everybody's looking at us!"

The Original
SINGAPORE SLING
Book

LANDMARK BOOKS PTE LTD

Editorial Note:
The editorial style of each contributor has been retained to show their perspectives. This includes the treatment and mis-spelling of Malay words by Colonial British writers.

Cover by Karen Hoisington

Typeset by Superskill Graphics Pte Ltd
Printed by Kim Hup Lee Printing Co. Pte Ltd

ISBN 981 3002 01 8 (hardback edition)
ISBN 981 3002 02 6 (paperback edition)

Contents

Publisher's Preface

RAFFLES Hotel's world-famous pink drink lends its name to this anthology about one of the most colourful places in the world.

This is an amusing and heady collection of over 25 pieces of writing about Singapore and its people, mixing elements of old and new in fiction and non-fiction, the sinister, the romantic, the witty and the profound. The panaroma takes you beyond ancient history, to mythical times and stretching onward to super-state Singapore. In between, chuckle at the foibles of the colonial Whites and feel the moods of War. Laugh with the superstitious Babas, swing to the rhythms of Singapore, relive its old ways and join a foodie tour. The best of Singapore authors have been commissioned to contribute their talents: Paik Choo, Ilsa Sharp, Siva Choy, Jacintha Abisheganaden, Yvonne Quahe, Violet Oon, Hugh Mabbett, Sit Yin Fong, Kathleen Chopard, Ovidia Yu... They are joined by British writers of the past, among them Maugham, Ommanney and Hugh Wilkinson.

This is an open-where-you-may, read-as-you-please book, a dip bag with no booby prizes, but not a few surprises. It's a bed-side book, a coffee-break book, a between class read, an airplane companion. A real entertainer.

Beyond that, sit back enjoy the cadances that echo from page to page, the mix of flavours that blend the individual pieces together into a unique insider's view of Singapore.

THE PLANTER'S LAMENT.

(with apologies to Jack Smith, America's Whispering Baritone)

"I'm knee deep in Lallang and
head over heels in Debt."

HOW TO BE A RUBBER PLANTER
by Hevea

FORTY-SEVEN years ago the first rubber seeds were taken from the Amazon and planted in British territory, yet any proprietor or estate manager in Malaya will tell you that planters are born, not made. They seem quite certain of this. The signs they say are obvious and are first noticeable in the nursery where the embryo planter should show a marked preference for a weak solution of latex to any form of patent milk foods. Later he is bound to forsake the delights of a rattle for a handful of rubber seeds, but the real crisis comes when, as a boy, he bounces his first sorbo ball. From that moment the die is cast, and he probably walks over to where his father is dozing by the fireside, sloshes him one over the eye, and exclaims "Say Dad, I'm going to be a planter." If at the same time he tosses off the remains of the glass of hot toddy by his parent's side, you may be quite certain that in a few years time the youth will be well on the way to fame and fortune.

Unfortunately, however, I'm afraid there are not enough "born" planters to meet the ever-growing demand in Malaya, so for the benefit of those who are not so fortunate, yet feel the call stirring within them, I propose to give a few hints of a useful and practical nature.

1. Before leaving home a youth should go to Kew Gardens and have a good look at the first rubber tree, which was planted there, I understand, in the year 1879. This tree is the ancestor of all the rubber trees in Malaya, and if he likes the look of it one of the beginner's chief difficulties will have been surmounted.

2. In the rubber business the sense of smell is of much greater importance than that of sight. The test for this is to take an old golf ball, unpick it carefully and − having previously bribed the cook − place the pickings in a saucepan and let them simmer gently for an hour over a slow fire. The advantages of doing this are twofold.

(a) The perpetrator of the offence will know that he can (or can't) endure the smells of a rubber factory without discomfort.

1

(b) Parents are liable to part with the passage money to Singapore with lighting rapidity, in order that the atrocity may not be repeated in the home.

3. Physical endurance is essential, but the following simple test is sufficient. Dress in some woollen underclothes, two pairs of flannel trousers, three sweaters and the heaviest overcoat obtainable, and walk round Kensington Gardens four times quickly on a wet August afternoon. On returning to domicile examine undergarments carefully for any sign of moisture. If they are still dry, or only slightly damp, the climate of Malaya is sure to be suitable.

4. Languages are useful, and a really good flow should be acquired early. The coolies of Malaya are imported from various parts of the world, so it is preferable to learn a few abusive terms in Chinese (various dialects), Javanese, Tamil and Hindustani. This may sound difficult at first, but it is possible to get a smattering sufficient for a beginner, in the parrot house of the Zoo.

So far I have only dealt with the purely technical side of the business, but the social side of a rubber planter's existence is of the greatest importance.

Everyone on a rubber plantation is a sportsman, because at any moment the white man may be confronted with tigers, elephants, rhinos or crocodiles. Guns for shooting these are cumbersome and expensive so they are usually supplied by the estate. The beginner should, however, bring out a small shotgun in the hope of some day bringing down a green pigeon, but it is advisable to have a clause inserted in the contract that should the gun go off at the wrong end, one's next-of-kin shall be informed. With regard to the tiger menace, a little practice in hard-staring is beneficial as a preliminary to facing the beast himself. Tigers are reputed to fear the steady gaze of man, and quite an inexpensive way of learning this valuable accomplishment is to spend a few Sunday mornings in Hyde Park, where it is reported, skirts are getting shorter every year. If a policeman should appear transfer the gaze to him.

SINGAPORE SLING

Tennis is a favourite game amongst planters. The standard of skill is very high, but novices need not be discouraged by this so long as they cultivate the correct procedure when playing mixed doubles. The ball is served into the net twice in rapid succession, and the server says "Sorry," it is then served twice over the back line, the player again chanting the word "Sorry" and so on, until the game ends. If the word "Sorry" is practised in various gradations to the accompaniment of a tuning fork, success is assured.

Dress for tennis is an important consideration. Care should be taken that the trousers are loose because shrinkage often occurs at the dhoby (laundry). Nothing can be more embarrassing than a sudden bursting of the seat when playing with the manager's wife. For this the word "Sorry," is not sufficient, as she is unlikely to have any safety pins available.

Very little further advice is necessary. Avoid brokers. Invest all savings in tin, or some commodity other than rubber. Purchase a pair of soft-soled shoes for office use, so as not to wake the manager in the afternoons. Learn a capacity for absorbing various forms of liquid (this can best be done during the voyage as there are usually expert instructors available on every ship.) Cultivate small talk (ditto).

Finally the beginner should seek advice from those with experience. He should try to do his colleagues' work as well as his own. They will be delighted to watch him do it.

from Straits Produce *(1926)*

3

CONFESSIONS OF A BAR BOY
by T. G. Ryott

MY name is Ahmat bin Haji Said, and I am Head Bar Boy at the Club. After passing the 3rd standard with great credit to the Guru and myself I served a very strenuous apprenticeship as punkah puller, tennis-ball-picker-up, peon, cleaner, fitter, unlicensed driver of a Ford car, rubber tapper and gharry driver. I finally decided on an indoor life, hung round the Club and eventually gained an entrée. I have been installed in my present position for about a year and feel fairly safe. A Bar Boy's life is full of ups and downs and I get a good many more kicks than half pence. It is always my fault if a glass gets broken, if the electric light is left burning all night, if the billiard chalk gives out, or water finds its way into the whisky. I suppose the next thing the Tuans will do is to cut my gaji if the papers are put in the covers the wrong way up, and they haven't the sense to see that they need only turn the papers up the other way but expect me to take them out and put them in again. I didn't go to the High School and they can't expect me to read English; they can't read Malay. I don't quite know how old I am but I am the proud possessor of a wife and eight children if that is any indication to my age; after all, there are worse jobs than being a Bar Boy and I have been able to invest in a Monopole Bicycle out of my savings on which I ride to the Club every morning from the Kampong in Banda Hilir. My diary for the day is something like this:—

7.30 a.m. Arrive at the Club on

the Monopole. Try to persuade the Kabun to carry Monopole up the steps, which he refuses to do. So do it myself: trip over the bar at the doorway, which said Kabun has failed to remove: have an altercation with him, and threaten to report him to the Secretary: put bicycle in a place of safety. By the way, I wonder how much longer the lynx-eyed Secretary will allow me to bring it inside the Club. Never heard of a Club before within the sacred portals of which bicycles were allowed to be introduced: walk round the bar in a leisurely way: help myself to a Three Castle Cigarette: open a window, put a chair on the verandah, change the calendar — 7.45 a.m. Arrival of Assistant Secretary: juggle with the Three Castle and yesterday's chits: general confusion and providential disappearance of cigarette: summoned by Assistant Secretary to inspect rhododendrons which have been depredated by the goats: refer him to the Kabun, and incidentally open old sores. 8 a.m. Arrival of Secretary: alarums and excursions with chairs, windows, billiard table brushes, globe polishing the foot-

rail and reproofs to the other boys. Summoned before Secretary: told to economise the whisky and mend the beer engine: strict instructions not to tamper with pianola and weighing machine. 9 a.m. Departure of Secretary and Assistant: heave a sigh of relief: altercation with Dollah: tell him I'm not here to blow up footballs and oil long-suffering cricket bats: I don't like Dollah: every man in his own sphere, I say. 9.15. Go home to makan nasi; 10.30, back again: monotony relieved by Salleh, Tuan A's boy, who has come for the Tuan's tennis racquet; Salleh is rather pandei and reads English, so we inspect the complaint book. No. 1 "Left my blazer here last night with two cents in the pocket: came next morning: blazer safe, money missing: cannot something be done to stop this petty pilfering by the club servants?" Name indecipherable as usual. No. 2 "11 a.m. and Head Bar Boy wrapped in the arms of Morpheus; no wonder the profits are going down; R" — rest illegible. Don't know what this means: never wrap myself in anything unless it is a blanket when I get fever. No. 3 "No chalk in the Billiard Room: suggest that Head Boy be told not to sell it to Dollah for marking out the tennis courts." To accuse me of stealing chalk is bad enough, but to suggest collusion with Dollah puts what they call the lid on it. Think I shall resign, but on second thoughts decide otherwise. No. 4; "Please impress on the boy to watch the signing of the chits: payment for drinks could not then be evaded." Signature as usual, but in addition "one who always pays." He may pay, but Dollah says he doesn't know much about English Grammar: this was quite uninteresting to me and the other remarks were still more feeble, so Salleh and I smoked Three Castles (they are much nicer than "Cycle") till 12 o'clock.

12 noon. Arrival of Salleh's Tuan: wants to know what Salleh is doing as he has finished office for the day (oh! these hard working Tuans) and wants to be off to Jasin. Ingenious excuse that there were many racquets and that he had been trying hard to pick out the right one; departure of Tuan and discomfiture of Salleh; enter the thirsty ones; shouts of "Boy" and imperious requests for Gin Slings: always the same old crowd and always the same remarks made to me in unintelligible Malay about the smallness of the measure and the nauseating taste of the beverage; if they don't like the taste of the drinks why don't they get their stores elsewhere and not accuse me of adulterating them with cigarette ash, grits, mosquitoes, onions or billiard chalk. However, they seem to get through a good many in spite of my evil intentioned efforts to poison them and they seldom leave me in peace before 1.30, when they go home to tiffin and probably treat their own boys in the same cavalier style. 1.30. Best part of the day except on Saturdays when they play a wretched game called cricket. Tell the Chinese boy to jaga: retire to the billiard room to lounge, make a pillow out of the table cloth and have a lovely sleep to prepare me for the hard work of the day. Wake up refreshed and at peace with Dollah, the Kabun, the Assistant Secretary and the world in general.

If there is one thing I loathe it is tennis tournaments, because of the extra work involved. Tennis has always been a bug-bear to me; there is such a lot of it. Without it I could be at ease till it got dark, for the cricketers, footballers and billiard players don't trouble me much till then. But oh! those tennis players: my life isn't my own after 5.30, and the ladies drink lime squashes in the same proportion as the men drink beers. They are so inconsiderate about it, too; you would think we kept lime squash on tap to hear their imperious remarks to me about being quick. Those are the days on which I earn my ridiculous gaji a dozen times over. Then the country folks imagine they can play tennis although they never walk off with prizes, and their motors have a nasty habit of not breaking down when the tournament is in progress: this all adds to my responsibility. Then, at about 6.30 to 7, when the tennis players have cleared off, the devotees of gin and whisky keep me fairly busy till 8.30 when they go home to dinner, and I follow their example.

I have often heard tell of Saturday night in an English Pub., but it must be as nothing compared to one in the Singapore Club on the occasion of a Lodge Night or a Dance. On a Lodge Night, all the respectable male inhabitants put on a black uniform, are very polite to each other and then adjourn to a house without windows. The outside world, which includes myself, is not supposed to know what goes on in that house but it must be pretty thirsty work judging from the amount they drink when they arrive back at the Club. The strange part of it is that the great majority are orang tuas, but be that as it may, they have to put up with a lot of good humoured banter from the young ones and hide their confusion by a multitude of drinks. They get home eventually with crumpled shirts and collars and somewhat aroma-

tic clothes. Lodge Night is so objectionable to me because it brings together people who have not met for about a month: doesn't seem very long, but provides a good excuse for just one more drink. I once took the trouble to count and found they had twenty just one more drinks. I get no extra pay or at least none worth considering for all the extra work I do, while the club may make anything extra up to fifty dollars.

Then I fairly hate what they call dances. It is as much as I can do to scrape a hari besar at the end of the fasting month, good Mohammedan that I am, but these Europeans must make a fuss whenever they get the slightest excuse. No doubt the reason why they divide themselves into three bangsas is that they can have three times as many hari besars. I think they call themselves North, South and West, just to save their faces. I was quaking in my shoes the end of last year but, after all, the men from the north played a very shabby trick on their fellow countrymen and met in the Club by themselves. I was distinctly relieved and gave thanks to Allah, because rubber was still falling. But the dances are very strange affairs: as a rule the Tuans dress much the same as they do on Lodge Nights while the mems quite shock my sense of decency. They come to the Club at the time when I am usually going to shut up. The forward ones embrace each other and then start twisting round the room while some other people are making an awful din which is called music. I would just as soon listen to the Chetty band at the Tamil festival. But they all seem very fond of the music, because as soon as it stops they sit down. The Tuans stand at the top of the stairs and watch for about half an hour, then they descend to the bar and my turn comes. I am kept hard at it — till about 3 a.m. You see, a lot of them have to wait for their wives who seem to like embracing some of the Tuans more than their husbands, the excuse being that the latter cannot dance. So there is nothing for the grass widowers to do but drink — billiards and cards are only side shows and all the work falls on me and the Chinese boy. Even if we do get a spare moment somebody wants lime squashes or claret for the ladies. And I am expected to see that everybody signs their chits and drinks what they have ordered! Supposing you try the effect of being confronted with a row of fifty hot flushed faces surmounting shirts collars and ties in a transition stage asking for drinks in thick, throaty tones of European Malay; why, it would be easier under the circumstances to build the Tower of Babel than to satisfy the cravings of these excitable revellers.

But they must get very tired of their own company, for sometimes they have a dance and pretend they are other people. The Tuans think they are women, soldiers, sailors, Frenchmen, clowns, mata matas and others whose names I don't know, and the ladies try to look like men, stars, tennis racquets and things of that kind. I don't suppose any of them know who each other is — they are all so stupid — but I can soon see through all their disguises. But whether they are dressed up or not they all get just as thirsty. Thank goodness, orgies of this kind only happen a few times

in a year or I should soon be back again in that Ford Car.

But you cannot be a Bar Boy for long without becoming a great anthropologist. "By their drinks ye shall know them" is the pantun which I drum into every new assistant. Everybody knows that ladies drink lime squashes, but I know the men who drink whisky, those who prefer beer and those who favour gin, and I can give them what they want before they ask for it. I know all the cautious men who don't sign their names to chits in the place indicated in case the Bar Boy (who can't read or write English, mind you) might have a drink and insinuate the same into the blank space; I know the iconoclasts, and the shady characters who forget to sign their chits or adorn them with indecipherable caligraphy; I know the firms who fatten at the Club's expense and I know the secret history of many committee meetings. I could tell you of black-ballings, resignations, expulsions, threatenings and slaughters; but my lips are tied — I am a servant of the Tuans.

And then, when I have poured

out the last stengah, turned off the last light (providentially) and fastened the Yale Lock, I ride back to the Kampong and ponder on the eccentricities of the European. Why he comes to the East is a conundrum, but even if I went to his country I can't imagine it would be possible for me to appear quite as big a fool.

from Gula Malacca *(1914)*

Immaculate one to sun-burnt planters :—Gentlemen, your presence is objectionable.
Begone before I stop the orchestra!

A REAL TIGER HUNT
by Alexander Powell

THE tiger is to Johore what the elephant is to Siam and the kangaroo to Australia – a sort of national trademark. Even the postage stamps bear an engraving of the striped monarch of the jungle. There is no place in the world, so far as I am aware, save only a zoo, of course, where one can get a shot at a tiger so quickly and with such minimum of effort. In this connection I heard a story at the Singapore Club, the truth of which is vouched for by those with whom I was having tiffin. Shortly before the war, it seems, an American business man who had amassed a fortune in the export business, and who was noted even in down-town New York as a hustler, was returning from a business trip to China. In the smoking-room of the homeward bound liner, over the highballs and cigars, he listened to the stories of an Englishman who had been hunting big game in Asia. The conversation eventually turned to tigers.

"Johore's the place for tigers," the Englishman remarked, pouring himself another peg of whiskey. "The beggars are as thick as foxes in Leicestershire. You're jolly well certain of bagging one the first day out."

"I've always wanted a tiger skin for my smoking room," commented the American. "Could buy one at a fur shop on the Avenue, of course, but I want one that I shot myself. Think I'll run over to Johore while we're at Singapore and get one."

"But I say, my dear fellow," expostulated the Briton, "you really can't do that, you know. We only stop at Singapore for half a day – get in at daybreak and leave again at noon. You can't get a tiger in that time."

"There's no such thing as 'can't' in my business. Business methods will bring results in tiger shooting as quickly as in anything else," retorted the American, rising and heading for the wireless room.

A few hours later the American's representative in Singapore, a youngster who had himself been

11

educated in the school of American business, received a wireless message from the head of his house. It read: "Arriving Singapore daybreak Thursday. Leaving noon same day. Wish to shoot tiger in Johore. Make arrangements."

Now the representative in Singapore knew perfectly well that his promotion, if not his job, depended upon his employer getting a tiger. And, as the steamer was due in four days, there was no time to spare. From the director of the Singapore zoo he purchased for considerably above the market price, a decrepit and somewhat moth-eaten tiger of advanced years, which he had transported across the straits to Johore, whence it was conveyed by bullock cart to a spot in the edge of the jungle, a dozen miles outside the town, where it was turned loose in an enclosure of wire and bamboo hastily constructed for the purpose.

When the steamer bearing the American magnate dropped anchor in the harbour, the local representative went aboard with the quarantine officer. Ten mi-

nutes later, thanks to arrangements made in advance, a launch was bearing him and his chief to the shore, where a motor car was waiting. It is barely a dozen miles from the wharf at Singapore to Woodlands, the ferry station opposite Johore, and the driver had orders to shatter the speed laws. A waiting launch streaked across the two miles of channel which separates the island from the mainland and drew up alongside the quay at Johore, where another car was waiting. The roads are excellent in the sultanate, and thirty minutes of fast driving brought the two Americans to the zareba, within which the tiger, guarded by natives, was peacefully breakfasting on a goat.

"He's a real man-eater," whispered the agent, handing his employer a loaded express rifle. "We only located him yesterday. Lured him with a goat, you know ... the smell of blood attracts 'em. You'd better put a bullet in him before he sees us. One just behind the shoulder will do the business."

The magnate, trembling with excitement for the first time in his busy life, drew bead on the tawny stripe behind the tiger's shoulder. There was a shattering roar, the great beast pawed convulsively at the air, then rolled on its side and lay motionless.

"Good work," the local man commented approvingly, "It's only an hour and forty minutes since we left the boat – a record for tiger shooting, I fancy. We'll be back at Raffles for breakfast by nine o'clock and after that I'll show you round the city. Don't worry about the skin, Sir. The natives'll tend to the skinning and I'll have it on board before you sail."

Now – so the story goes – after dinner in the magnate's New York home he takes his guests into the smoking room for cigars and coffee. Spread before the fireplace is a great orange and black pelt, a trifle faded it is true, but indubitably the skin of a tiger.

"Yes," the host complacently in reply to his guests' admiring comments, "a real man-eater. Shot him myself in the Johore jungle. Easy enough to get a tiger if you use American business methods."

from Where the Strange Trails Go Down (1921)

Oh Those Tiger TALES !

13

PURE ENGLISH
by M. W.

THE WORST of going Home after a long spell out East is the irritating way people have of asking you to explain your pet phrases. Its a perfect nuisance to have to think of words for "chit," "barang," or "stengah."

My sister says in a superior tone that English is good enough for her, and why can't I say "comfortable" if I mean "comfortable," instead of talking about being "senang"?

I ask you? Is it the same?

And then lunch!

Such a stuffy meal — but call it "tiffin" and you feel brighter at once.

But you can't explain! They won't listen. All they'll do is to invent silly chaff.

"Let's see," says my young brother with a fatuous grin as we sit down "Is this Pitchin, or Tuckin, or Fillin?"

The funny thing is the way you fearlessly determine to air your French when you land at Marseilles, and find you can only talk Malay.

You babble at the blue-bloused porter, who stands, your suit case in his hand, waiting your commands —

"Ankat itu, taroh dalam Taxi"!

He gazes spell-bound.

He knows quite well you are English. If he is a nice fellow he doesn't break it to you that he knows your language, but if the garlic has disagreed with him, or the morning snails were not up to standard, he says sharply:

"Hein?"

That tears it. You feel an utter fool.

"All right," you say "piggi customs. Where is it? Sini?"

And only after a time do you realise you are still floundering in Malay. Still that's France. And you can't expect them to understand.

What a relief to go to the club and meet a fellow exile! "What'll you have, old chap?" he asks, "a stengah?"

14

It tastes about twice as good as the whiskey and soda Uncle offered yesterday.

I met an old bore — friend of the family — the other day in Bond Street. He prides himself on never using a foreign word if there is an English equivalent. We had a conversation something like this:

He — "Hallo! What are you doing here? On leave? Or business?"

Me — "Oh! Just a makan angin, don't you know."

He — "Eh?"

Me — "Home-leave — holiday, Sir."

He — "Ah! Yes. You've been out in Malaya, haven't you?"

Me — "Yes, Sir. I've a Klapa Kebun out there."

He — "Eh?"

Me — "A Klapa Estate...er...Coconut Plantation."

He — "Oh! Ah! Yes—very interesting. Profitable?"

Me — "So, so! I make about $1,000 a month."

He — "Thousand dollars a month. Let me see, how many dollars go to the pound?"

Me — "Eight-fifty, or thereabouts."

He — "So really you make—as much as (he calculated slowly but I did not help him) £130 a month?"

Me — "Well, not quite as much as that. Eight-fifty you know."

He — "Oh! Ah! Yes, — gross, of course?"

Me (wilfully misunderstanding) — "The gross? No, we sell them in catties and piculs."

He (laughing uneasily) — "Pickles? I had no idea you made pickles out of coconuts."

Me (wickedly) — "Yes. There are a lot of piculs in Singapore — the Chinese deal extensively in them."

He (deeply interested) — "Do they indeed? Have you a factory then?"

Me — "Oh yes. We dry the copra in the sun, and then picul it in."

He (not quite clear) — "In what?"

Me — "In baskets."

He — "Pickles in baskets! How extraordinary!"

Me — "Yes, its a funny custom but we all do it."

He (Giving it up) — "And how long are you over for?"

Me — "About six months, unless I get fed up. Then I shall pack up my barang, and "pulong balek" as they say in Malay."

He (earnestly advising an old friend's son) — "Never get into the habit of using foreign words, my dear Alfred. When there is an English equivalent use it, my dear boy, use it!"

Me (desperate) — "Yes, sir, Well, I think I must be getting along now, if you'll excuse ....

He (most affable) — "Yes, Yes — au revoir, Alfred, au revoir!"

"GOOD-BYE," I said with emphasis.

After all the English language is good enough for me, on occasions.

(*Scene:* The Gare du Nord. Calais Express just leaving).
Planter on leave (in serious trouble with his luggage): "Ou est satu orang buleh parle Anglais!"

16

THE LETTER

by Somerset Maugham

OUTSIDE on the quay the sun beat fiercely. A stream of motors, lorries and buses, private cars and hirelings, sped up and down the crowded thoroughfare, and every chauffeur blew his horn; rickshaws threaded their nimble path amid the throng, and the panting coolies found breath to yell at one another; coolies, carrying heavy bales, sidled along with their quick jog-trot and shouted to the passer-by to make way; itinerant vendors proclaimed their wares. Singapore is the meeting-place of a hundred peoples; and men of all colours, black Tamils, yellow Chinks, brown Malays, Armenians, Jews and Bengalis, called to one another in raucous tones. But inside the office of Messrs. Ripley, Joyce and Naylor it was pleasantly cool; it was dark after the dusty glitter of the street and agreeably quiet after its unceasing din. Mr. Joyce sat in his private room, at the table, with an electric fan turned full on him. He was leaning back, his elbows on the arms of the chair, with the tips of the outstretched fingers of one hand resting neatly against the tips of the outstretched fingers of the other. His gaze rested on the battered volumes of the Law Reports which stood on a long shelf in front of him. On the top of a cupboard were square boxes of japanned tin, on which were painted the names of various clients.

There was a knock at the door.

"Come in."

A Chinese clerk, very neat in his white ducks, opened it.

"Mr. Crosbie is here, sir."

He spoke beautiful English, accenting each word with precision, and Mr. Joyce had often wondered at the extent of his vocabulary. Ong Chi Seng was a Cantonese, and he had studied law at Gray's Inn. He was spending a year or two with Messrs. Ripley, Joyce and Naylor in order to prepare himself for practise on his own account. He was industrious, obliging, and of exemplary character.

"Show him in," said Mr. Joyce.

He rose to shake hands with his visitor and asked him to sit down. The light fell on him as he did so. The face of Mr. Joyce remained in shadow. He was by nature a silent man, and now he looked at Robert Crosbie for quite a minute without speaking. Crosbie was a big fellow, well over six feet high, with broad shoulders, and muscular. He was a rubber-planter, hard with the constant exercise of walking over the estate, and with the tennis which was his relaxation when the day's work was over. He was deeply sunburned. His hairy hands, his feet in clumsy boots, were enormous, and Mr. Joyce found himself thinking that a blow of that great fist would easily kill the fragile Tamil. But there was no fierceness in his blue eyes; they were confiding and gentle; and his face, with its big, undistinguished features, was open, frank and honest. But at this moment it bore a look of deep distress. It was drawn and haggard.

"You look as though you hadn't had much sleep the last night or two," said Mr. Joyce.

"I haven't."

Mr. Joyce noticed now the old felt hat, with its broad double brim, which Crosbie had placed on the table; and then his eyes travelled to the khaki shorts he wore, showing his red hairy thighs, the tennis shirt open at the neck, without a tie, and the dirty khaki jacket with the ends of the sleeves turned up. He looked as though he had just come in from a long tramp among the rubber trees. Mr. Joyce gave a slight frown.

"You must pull yourself together, you know. You must keep your head."

"Oh, I'm all right."

"Have you seen your wife to-day?"

"No, I'm to see her this afternoon. You know, it is a damned shame that they should have arrested her."

"I think they had to do that," Mr. Joyce answered in his level, soft tone.

"I should have thought they'd have let her out on bail."

"It's a very serious charge."

"It is damnable. She did what any decent woman would do in her place. Only, nine women out of ten wouldn't have the pluck. Leslie's the best woman in the world. She wouldn't hurt a fly. Why, hang it all, man, I've been married to her for twelve years, do you think I don't know her? God, if I'd got hold of the man I'd have wrung his neck, I'd have killed him without a moment's hesitation. So would you."

"My dear fellow, everybody's on your side. No one has a good word to say for Hammond. We're going to get her off. I don't suppose either the assessors or the judge will go into court without having already made up their minds to bring in a verdict of not guilty."

"The whole thing's a farce," said Crosbie violently. "She ought never to have been arrested in the first place, and then it's terrible, after all the poor girl's gone through, to subject her to the ordeal of a trial. There's not a soul I've met since I've been in Singapore, man or woman, who hasn't told me that Leslie was absolutely justified. I think it's awful to keep her in prison all these weeks."

"The law is the law. After all, she confesses that she killed the man. It is terrible, and I'm dreadfully sorry for both you and for her."

"I don't matter a hang," interrupted Crosbie.

"But the fact remains that murder has been committed, and in a civilised community a trial is inevitable."

"Is it murder to exterminate noxious vermin? She shot him as she would have shot a mad dog."

Mr. Joyce leaned back again in his chair and once more placed the tips of his ten fingers together. The little construction he formed looked like the skeleton of a roof. He was silent for a moment.

"I should be wanting in my duty as your legal adviser," he said at last, in an even voice, looking at his client with his cool, brown eyes, "if I did not tell you that there is one point which causes me just a little anxiety.

If your wife had only shot Hammond once, the whole thing would be absolutely plain sailing. Unfortunately she fired six times."

"Her explanation is perfectly simple. In the circumstances anyone would have done the same."

"I daresay," said Mr. Joyce, "and of course I think the explanation is very reasonable. But it's no good closing our eyes to the facts. It's always a good plan to put yourself in another man's place, and I can't deny that if I were prosecuting for the Crown that is the point on which I should centre my enquiry."

"My dear fellow, that's perfectly idiotic."

Mr. Joyce shot a sharp glance at Robert Crosbie. The shadow of a smile hovered over his shapely lips. Crosbie was a good fellow, but he could hardly be described as intelligent.

"I daresay it's of no importance," answered the lawyer, "I just thought it was a point worth mentioning. You haven't got very long to wait now, and when it's all over I recommend you to go off somewhere with your wife on a trip, and forget all about it. Even though we are almost dead certain to get an acquittal, a trial of that sort is anxious work, and you'll both want a rest."

For the first time Crosbie smiled, and his smile strangely changed his face. You forgot the uncouthness and saw only the goodness of his soul.

"I think I shall want it more than Leslie. She's borne up wonderfully. By God, there's a plucky little woman for you."

"Yes, I've been very much struck by her self-control," said the lawyer. "I should never have guessed that she was capable of such determination."

His duties as her counsel had made it necessary for him to have a good many interviews with Mrs. Crosbie since her arrest. Though things had been made as easy as could be for her, the fact remained that she was in jail, awaiting her trial for murder, and it would not have been surprising if her nerves had failed her. She appeared to bear her ordeal with composure. She read a great deal, took such exercise as was possible, and by favour of the authorities worked at the pillow lace which had always formed the entertainment of her long hours of leisure. When Mr. Joyce saw her, she was neatly dressed in cool, fresh, simple frocks, her hair was carefully arranged, and her nails were manicured. Her manner was collected. She was able even to jest upon the little inconveniences of her position. There was something casual about the way in which she spoke of the tragedy, which suggested to Mr. Joyce that only her good breeding prevented her from finding something a trifle ludicrous in a situation which was eminently serious. It surprised him, for he had never thought that she had a sense of humour.

He had known her off and on for a good many years. When she paid visits to Singapore she generally came to dine with his wife and himself, and once or twice she had passed a week-end with them at their bungalow by the sea. His wife had spent a fortnight with her on the estate, and had met Geoffrey Hammond several times. The two couples had been on friendly, if not on intimate, terms, and it was on this account that Robert Crosbie had rushed over to Singapore immediately after the catastrophe and begged Mr. Joyce to take charge personally of his unhappy wife's defence.

The story she told him the first time he saw her, she had never varied in the smallest detail. She told it as coolly then, a few hours after the tragedy, as she told it now. She told it connectedly, in a level, even voice, and her only sign of confusion was when a slight colour came into her cheeks as she described one or two of its incidents. She was the last woman to whom one would have expected such a thing to happen. She was in the early thirties, a fragile creature, neither short nor tall, and graceful rather than pretty. Her wrists and ankles were very delicate, but she was extremely thin, and you could see the bones of her hands through the white skin, and the veins were large and blue. Her face was colourless, slightly sallow, and her lips were pale. You did not notice the colour of her eyes. She had a great deal of light brown hair, and it had a slight natural wave; it was the sort of hair that with a little touching-up would have been very pretty, but you could not imagine that Mrs. Crosbie would think of resorting to any such device. She was

21

a quiet, pleasant, unassuming woman. Her manner was engaging, and if she was not very popular it was because she suffered from a certain shyness. This was comprehensible enough, for the planter's life is lonely, and in her own house, with people she knew, she was in her quiet way charming. Mrs. Joyce, after her fortnight's stay, had told her husband that Leslie was a very agreeable hostess. There was more in her, she said, than people thought; and when you came to know her you were surprised how much she had read and how entertaining she could be.

She was the last woman in the world to commit murder.

Mr. Joyce dismissed Robert Crosbie with such reassuring words as he could find and, once more alone in his office, turned over the pages of the brief. But it was a mechanical action, for all its details were familiar to him. The case was the sensation of the day, and it was discussed in all the clubs, at all the dinner tables, up and down the Peninsula, from Singapore to Penang.The facts that Mrs. Crosbie gave were simple. Her husband had gone to Singapore on business, and she was alone for the night. She dined by herself, late, at a quarter to nine, and after dinner sat in the sitting-room working at her lace. It opened on the verandah. There was no one in the bungalow, for the servants had retired to their own quarters at the back of the compound. She was surprised to hear a step on the gravel path in the garden, a booted step, which suggested a white man rather than a native, for she had not heard a motor drive up, and she could not imagine who could be coming to see her at that time of night. Someone ascended the few stairs that led up to the bungalow, walked across the verandah, and appeared at the door of the room in which she sat. At the first moment she did not recognise the visitor. She sat with a shaded lamp, and he stood with his back to the darkness.

"May I come in?" he said.

She did not even recognise the voice.

"Who is it?" she asked.

She worked with spectacles, and she took them off as she spoke.

SINGAPORE SLING

"Geoff. Hammond."

"Of course. Come in and have a drink."

She rose and shook hands with him cordially. She was a little surprised to see him, for though he was a neighbour neither she nor Robert had been lately on very intimate terms with him, and she had not seen him for some weeks. He was the manager of a rubber estate nearly eight miles from theirs, and she wondered why he had chosen this late hour to come and see them.

"Robert's away," she said, "He had to go to Singapore for the night."

Perhaps he thought his visit called for some explanation, for he said:

"I'm sorry. I felt rather lonely to-night, so I thought I'd just come along and see how you were getting on."

"How on earth did you come? I never heard a car."

"I left it down the road. I thought you might both be in bed and asleep."

This was natural enough. The planter gets up at dawn in order to take the roll-call of the workers, and soon after dinner he is glad to go to bed. Hammond's car was in point of fact found next day a quarter of a mile from the bungalow.

Since Robert was away there was no whisky and soda in the room. Leslie did not call the boy, who was probably asleep, but fetched it herself. Her guest mixed himself a drink and filled his pipe.

Geoff. Hammond had a host of friends in the colony. He was at this time in the late thirties, but he had come out as a lad. He had been one of the first to volunteer on the outbreak of war, and had done very well. A wound in the knee caused him to be invalided out of the army after two years, but he returned to the Federated Malay States with a D.S.O. and an M.C. He was one of the best billiard-players in the colony. He had been a beautiful dancer and a fine tennis player, but though able no longer to dance, and his tennis, with a stiff knee, was not so good as it had been, he had the gift of popularity and was universally liked. He was a tall, good-looking fellow, with attractive blue eyes and a fine head of black, curling hair. Old stagers said his only fault was that he was too fond of the girls, and after the catastrophe they shook their heads and vowed that they had always known this would get him into trouble.

He began now to talk to Leslie about the local affairs, the forthcoming races in Singapore, the price of rubber, and his chances of killing a tiger which had been lately seen in the neighbourhood. She was anxious to finish by a certain date the piece of lace on which she was working, for she wanted to send it home for her mother's birthday, and so put on her spectacles again, and drew towards her chair the little table on which stood the pillow.

"I wish you wouldn't wear those great horn-spectacles," he said. "I don't know why a pretty woman should do her best to look plain."

She was a trifle taken aback at this remark. He had never used that tone with her before. She thought the best thing was to make light for it.

"I have no pretensions to being a raving beauty, you know, and if you ask me point blank, I'm bound to tell you that I don't care two pins if you think me plain or not."

"I don't think you're plain. I think you're awfully pretty."

"Sweet of you," she answered, ironically. "But in that case I can only think you half-witted."

He chuckled. But he rose from his chair and sat down in another by her side.

"You're not going to have the face to deny that you have the prettiest hands in the world," he said.

He made a gesture as though to take one of them. She gave him a little tap.

"Don't be an idiot. Sit down where you were before and talk sensibly, or else I shall send you home."

He did not move.

"Don't you know that I'm awfully in love with you?" he said.

She remained quite cool.

"I don't. I don't believe it for a minute, and even if it were true I don't want you to say it."

She was the more surprised at what he was saying, since during the

24

seven years she had known him he had never paid her any particular attention. When he came back from the war they had seen a good deal of one another, and once when he was ill Robert had gone over and brought him back to their bungalow in his car. He had stayed with them then for a fortnight. But their interests were dissimilar, and the acquaintance had never ripened into friendship. For the last two or three years they had seen little of him. Now and then he came over to play tennis, now and then they met him at some planter's who was giving a party, but it often happened that they did not set eyes on him for a month at a time.

Now he took another whiskey and soda. Leslie wondered if he had been drinking before. There was something odd about him, and it made her a trifle uneasy. She watched him help himself with disapproval.

"I wouldn't drink any more if I were you," she said, good-humouredly still.

He emptied his glass and put it down.

"Do you think I'm talking to you like this because I'm drunk?" he asked abruptly.

"That is the most obvious explanation, isn't it?"

"Well, it's a lie. I've loved you ever since I first knew you. I've held my tongue as long as I could, and now it's got to come out. I love you, I love you, I love you."

She rose and carefully put aside the pillow.

"Good-night," she said.

"I'm not going now."

At last she began to lose her temper.

"But, you poor fool, don't you know that I've never loved anyone but Robert, and even if I didn't love Robert you're the last man I should care for."

"What do I care? Robert's away."

"If you don't go away this minute I shall call the boys, and have you thrown out."

"They're out of earshot."

She was very angry now. She made a movement as though to go on to the verandah from which the house-boy would certainly hear her, but he seized her arm.

"Let me go," she cried furiously.

"Not much. I've got you now."

She opened her mouth and called "Boy, boy," but with a quick gesture he put his hand over it. Then before she knew what he was about he had taken her in his arms and was kissing her passionately. She struggled, turning her lips away from his burning mouth.

"No, no, no," she cried. "Leave me alone. I won't."

She grew confused about what happened then. All that had been said before she remembered accurately, but now his words assailed her ears through a mist of horror and fear. He seemed to plead for her love. He broke into violent protestations of passion. And all the time he held her in his tempestuous embrace. She was helpless, for he was a strong, powerful man, and her arms were pinioned to her sides; her struggles were unavailing, and she felt herself grow weaker; she was afraid she would faint, and his hot breath on her face made her feel desperately sick. He kissed her mouth, her eyes, her cheeks, her hair. The pressure of his arms was killing her. He lifted her off her feet. She tried to kick him, but he only held her more closely. He was carrying her now. He wasn't speaking any more, but she knew that his face was pale and his eyes hot with desire. He was taking her into the bedroom. He was no longer a civilised man, but a savage. And as he ran he stumbled against a table which was in the way. His stiff knee made him a little awkward on his feet, and with the burden of the woman in his arms he fell. In a moment she had snatched herself away from him. She ran round the sofa. He was up in a flash, and flung himself towards her. There was a revolver on the desk. She was not a nervous woman, but Robert was to be away for the night, and she had meant to take it into her room when she went to bed. That was why it happened to be there. She was frantic with terror now. She did not know what she was doing. She heard a report. She saw Hammond stagger. He gave a cry. He said something, she didn't know what. He lurched out of the room on to the verandah. She was in a frenzy now, she was beside herself, she followed him out, yes, that was it, she must have followed him out, though she remembered nothing of it, she followed firing automatically shot after shot, till the six chambers were empty. Hammond fell down on the floor of the verandah. He crumpled up into a bloody heap.

When the boys, startled by the reports, rushed up, they found her standing over Hammond with the revolver still in her hand, and Hammond lifeless. She looked at them for a moment without speaking. They stood in a frightened, huddled bunch. She let the revolver fall from her hand, and without a word turned and went into the sitting-room. They watched her go into her bedroom and turn the key in the lock. They dared not touch the dead body, but looked at it with terrified eyes, talking excitedly to one another in undertones. Then the head-boy collected himself; he had been with them for many years, he was Chinese and a level-headed fellow. Robert had gone into Singapore on his motor-cycle, and the car stood in the garage. He told the syces to get it out; they must go at once to the Assissant District Officer and tell him what had happened. He picked up the revolver and put it in his pocket. The A.D.O., a man called Withers, lived on the outskirts of the nearest town, which was about thirty-five miles away. It took them an hour and a half to reach him. Everyone was asleep, and they had to rouse the boys. Presently Withers came out and they told him their errand. The head-boy showed him the revolver in proof of what he said. The A.D.O. went into his room to dress, sent for his car, and in a little while was following them back along the deserted road. The dawn was just breaking as he reached the Crosbie's bungalow. He ran up the steps of the verandah, and stopped short as he saw Hammond's body lying where he fell. He touched the face. It was quite cold.

"Where's mem?" he asked the house-boy.

The Chinese pointed to the bedroom. Withers went to the door and knocked. There was no answer. He knocked again.

"Mrs. Crosbie," he called.

"Who is it?"

"Withers."

There was another pause. Then the door was unlocked and slowly opened. Leslie stood before him. She had not been to bed, and wore the tea-gown in which she had dined. She stood and looked silently at the A.D.O.

"Your house-boy fetched me," he said, "Hammond. What have you done?"

"He tried to rape me, and I shot him."

"My God. I say, you'd better come out here. You must tell me exactly what happened."

"Not now. I can't. You must give me time. Send for my husband."

Withers was a young man, and he did not know exactly what to do in an emergency which was so out of the run of his duties. Leslie refused to say anything till at last Robert arrived. Then she told the two men the story, from which since then, though she had repeated it over and over again, she had never in the slightest degree diverged.

The point to which Mr. Joyce recurred was the shooting. As a lawyer he was bothered that Leslie had fired not once, but six times, and the examination of the dead man showed that four of the shots had been fired close to the body. One might almost have thought that when the man fell she stood over him and emptied the contents of the revolver into him. She confessed that her memory, so accurate for all that had preceded, failed her here. Her mind was blank. It pointed to an uncontrollable fury; but uncontrollable fury was the last thing you would have expected from this quiet and demure woman. Mr. Joyce had known her a good many years, and had always thought her an unemotional person; during the weeks that had passed since the tragedy her composure had been amazing.

Mr. Joyce shrugged his shoulders.

"The fact is, I suppose," he reflected, "that you can never tell what hidden possibilities of savagery there are in the most respectable of women."

There was a knock at the door.

"Come in."

The Chinese clerk entered and closed the door behind him. He closed it gently, with deliberation, but decidedly, and advanced to the table at which Mr. Joyce was sitting.

"May I trouble you, sir, for a few words of private conversation?" he said.

The elaborate accuracy with which the clerk expressed himself always faintly amused Mr. Joyce, and now he smiled.

"It's no trouble, Chi Seng," he replied.

"The matter on which I desire to speak to you, sir, is delicate and confidential.

"Fire away."

Mr. Joyce met his clerk's shrewd eyes. As usual Ong Chi Seng was dressed in the height of local fashion. He wore very shiny patent leather shoes and gay silk socks. In his black tie was a pearl and ruby pin, and on the fourth finger of his left hand a diamond ring. From the pocket of his neat white coat protruded a gold fountain pen and a gold pencil. He wore a gold wrist-watch, and on the bridge of his nose invisible pince-nez. He gave a little cough.

"The matter has to do with the case R. *v.* Crosbie, sir."

"Yes?"

"A circumstance has come to my knowledge, sir, which seems to me to put a different complexion on it."

"What circumstance?"

"It has come to my knowledge, sir, that there is a letter in existence from the defendant to the unfortunate victim of the tragedy."

"I shouldn't be at all surprised. In the course of the last seven years I have no doubt that Mrs. Crosbie often had occasion to write to Mr. Hammond."

Mr. Joyce had a high opinion of his clerk's intelligence and his words were designed to conceal his thoughts.

"That is very probable, sir. Mrs. Crosbie must have communicated with the deceased frequently, to invite him to dine with her for example, or to propose a tennis game. That was my first thought when the matter was brought to my notice. This letter, however, was written on the day of the late Mr. Hammond's death."

Mr. Joyce did not flicker an eyelash. He continued to look at Ong Chi Seng with the smile of faint amusement with which he generally talked to him.

"Who has told you this?"

"The circumstances were brought to my knowledge, sir, by a friend of mine."

Mr. Joyce knew better than to insist.

"You will no doubt recall, sir, that Mrs. Crosbie has stated that until the fatal night she had had no communication with the deceased for several weeks."

"Have you got the letter?"

"No, sir,"

"What are its contents?"

"My friend gave me a copy. Would you like to peruse it, sir?"

"I should."

Ong Chi Seng took from an inside pocket a bulky wallet. It was filled with papers, Singapore dollar notes and cigarette cards. From the confusion he presently extracted a half sheet of thin note-paper and placed it before Mr. Joyce. The letter read as follows:—

> R. *will be away for the night. I absolutely must see you. I*
> *shall expect you at eleven. I am desperate, and if you don't come*
> *I won't answer for the consequences. Don't drive up.*—L.

It was written in the flowing hand which the Chinese were taught at the foreign schools. The writing, so lacking in character, was oddly incongruous with the ominous words.

"What makes you think that this note was written by Mrs. Crosbie?"

"I have every confidence in the veracity of my informant, sir," replied Ong Chi Seng. "And the matter can very easily be put to the proof. Mrs. Crosbie will, no doubt, be able to tell you at once whether she wrote such a letter or not."

Since the beginning of the conversation Mr. Joyce had not taken his eyes off the respectable countenance of his clerk. He wondered now if he discerned in it a faint expression of mockery.

"It is inconceivable that Mrs. Crosbie should have written such a letter," said Mr. Joyce.

"If that is your opinion, sir, the matter is of course ended. My friend spoke to me on the subject only because he thought, as I was in your office, you might like to know of the existence of this letter before a communication was made to the Deputy Public Prosecutor."

"Who has the original?" asked Mr. Joyce sharply.

Ong Chi Seng made no sign that he perceived in this question and its manner a change of attitude.

"You will remember, sir, no doubt, that after the death of Mr. Hammond it was discovered that he had had relations with a Chinese woman. The letter is at present in her possession."

That was one of the things which had turned public opinion most vehemently against Hammond. It came to be known that for several months he had had a Chinese woman living in his house.

For a moment neither of them spoke. Indeed everything had been said and each understood the other perfectly.

"I'm obliged to you, Chi Seng. I will give the matter my consideration."

"Very good, sir. Do you wish me to make a communication to that effect to my friend?"

"I daresay it would be as well if you kept in touch with him," Mr. Joyce answered with gravity.

"Yes, sir."

The clerk noiselessly left the room, shutting the door again with deliberation, and left Mr. Joyce to his reflections. He stared at the copy, in its neat, impersonal writing, of Leslie's letter. Vague suspicions troubled him. They were so disconcerting that he made an effort to put them out of his mind. There must be a simple explanation of the letter, and Leslie without doubt could give it at once, but, by heaven, an explanation was needed. He rose from his chair, put the letter in his pocket, and took his topee. When he went out Ong Chi Seng was busily writing at his desk.

"I'm going out for a few minutes, Chi Seng," he said.

"Mr. George Reed is coming by appointment at twelve o'clock, sir. Where shall I say you've gone?"

Mr. Joyce gave him a thin smile.

"You can say that you haven't the least idea."

But he knew perfectly well that Ong Chi Seng was aware that he was going to the jail. Though the crime had been committed in Belanda and the trial was to take place at Belanda Bharu, since there was in the jail no convenience for the detention of a white woman Mrs. Crosbie had been brought to Singapore.

When she was led into the room in which he waited she held out her thin, distinguished hand, and gave him a pleasant smile. She was as ever neatly and simply dressed, and her abundant, pale hair was arranged with care.

"I wasn't expecting to see you this morning," she said, graciously.

She might have been in her own house, and Mr. Joyce almost expected to hear her call the boy and tell him to bring the visitor a gin pahit.

"How are you?" he asked.

"I'm in the best of health, thank you." A flicker of amusement flashed across her eyes. "This is a wonderful place for a rest cure."

The attendant withdrew and they were left alone.

"Do sit down," said Leslie.

He took a chair. He did not quite know how to begin. She was so cool that it seemed almost impossible to say to her the thing he had come to say. Though she was not pretty there was something agreeable in her appearance. She had elegance, but it was the elegance of good breeding in which there was nothing of the artifice of society. You had only to look at her to know what sort of people she had known and what kind of surroundings she had lived in. Her fragility gave her a singular refinement. It was impossible to associate her with the vaguest idea of grossness.

"I'm looking forward to seeing Robert this afternoon," she said, in her good-humoured, easy voice. (It was a pleasure to hear her speak, her voice and her accent were so distinctive of her class.) "Poor dear, it's been a great trial to his nerves. I'm thankful it'll all be over in a few days."

"It's only five days now."

"I know. Each morning when I awake I say to myself, 'one less.'" She smiled then. "Just as I used to do at school and the holidays were coming."

"By the way, am I right in thinking that you had no communication whatever with Hammond for several weeks before the catastrophe?"

"I'm quite positive of that. The last time we met was at a tennis-party at the MacFarrens. I don't think I said more than two words to him. They have two courts, you know, and we didn't happen to be in the same sets."

"And you haven't written to him?"

"Oh, no."

"Are you quite sure of that?"

"Oh, quite," she answered, with a little smile. "There was nothing I should write to him for except to ask him to dine or to play tennis, and I hadn't done either for months."

"At one time you'd been on fairly intimate terms with him. How did it happen that you had stopped asking him to anything?"

Mrs. Crosbie shrugged her thin shoulders.

"One gets tired of people. We hadn't anything very much in common. Of course, when he was ill Robert and I did everything we could for him, but the last year or two he'd been quite well, and he was very popular. He had a good many calls on his time, and there didn't seem to be any need to shower invitations upon him."

"Are you quite certain that was all?"

Mrs. Crosbie hesitated for a moment.

"Well, I may just as well tell you. It had come to our ears that he was living with a Chinese woman, and Robert said he wouldn't have him in the house. I had seen her myself."

Mr. Joyce was sitting in a straight-backed armchair, resting his chin on his hand, and his eyes were fixed on Leslie. Was it his fancy that, as she made this remark, her black pupils were filled on a sudden, for the fraction of a second, with a dull red light? The effect was startling. Mr. Joyce shifted in his chair. He placed the tips of his ten fingers together. He spoke very slowly, choosing his words.

"I think I should tell you that there is in existence a letter in your handwriting to Geoff. Hammond."

He watched her closely. She made no movement, nor did her face change colour, but she took a noticeable time to reply.

"In the past I've often sent him little notes to ask him to something or other, or to get me something when I knew he was going to Singapore."

"This letter asks him to come and see you because Robert was going to Singapore."

"That's impossible. I never did anything of the kind."

"You'd better read it for yourself."

He took it out of his pocket and handed it to her. She gave it a glance and with a smile of scorn handed it back to him.

"That's not my handwriting."

"I know, it's said to be an exact copy of the original."

She read the words now, and as she read a horrible change came over her. Her colourless face grew dreadful to look at. It turned green. The flesh seemed on a sudden to fall away and her skin was tightly stretched over the bones. Her lips receded, showing her teeth, so that she had the appearance of making a grimace. She stared at Mr. Joyce with eyes that started from their sockets. He was looking now at a gibbering death's head.

"What does it mean?" she whispered.

Her mouth was so dry that she could utter no more than a hoarse sound. It was no longer a human voice.

"That is for you to say," he answered.

"I didn't write it. I swear I didn't write it."

"Be very careful what you say. If the original is in your handwriting it would be useless to deny it."

"It would be a forgery."

"It would be difficult to prove that. It would be easy to prove that it was genuine."

A shiver passed through her lean body. But great beads of sweat stood on her forehead. She took a handkerchief from her bag and wiped the palms of her hands. She glanced at the letter again and gave Mr. Joyce a sidelong look.

"It's not dated. If I had written it and forgotten all about it, it might have been written years ago. If you'll give me time, I'll try and remember the circumstances."

"I noticed there was no date. If this letter were in the hands of the prosecution they would cross-examine the boys. They would soon find out whether someone took a letter to Hammond on the day of his death."

Mrs. Crosbie clasped her hands violently and swayed in her chair so that he thought she would faint.

"I swear to you that I didn't write that letter."

Mr. Joyce was silent for a little while. He took his eyes from her distraught face, and looked down on the floor. He was reflecting.

"In these circumstances we need not go into the matter further," he said slowly, at last breaking the silence. "If the possesser of this letter sees fit to place it in the hands of the prosecution you will be prepared."

His words suggested that he had nothing more to say to her, but he made no movement of departure. He waited. To himself he seemed to wait a very long time. He did not look at Leslie, but he was conscious that she sat very still. She made no sound. At last it was he who spoke.

"If you have nothing more to say to me I think I'll be getting back to my office."

35

"What would anyone who read the letter be inclined to think that it meant?" she asked then.

"He'd know that you had told a deliberate lie," answered Mr. Joyce sharply.

"When?"

"You have stated definitely that you had had no communication with Hammond for at least three months."

"The whole thing has been a terrible shock to me. The events of that dreadful night have been a nightmare. It's not very strange if one detail has escaped my memory."

"It would be unfortunate when your memory has reproduced so exactly every particular of your interview with Hammond, that you should have forgotten so important a point as that he came to see you in the bungalow on the night of his death at your express desire."

"I hadn't forgotten. After what happened I was afraid to mention it. I thought none of you'd believe my story if I admitted that he'd come at my invitation. I daresay it was stupid of me; but I lost my head, and after I'd said once that I'd had no communication with Hammond I was obliged to stick to it."

By now Leslie had recovered her admirable composure, and she met Mr. Joyce's appraising glance with candour. Her gentleness was very disarming.

"You will be required to explain, then, *why* you asked Hammond to come and see you when Robert was away for the night."

She turned her eyes full on the lawyer. He had been mistaken in thinking them insignificant, they were rather fine eyes, and unless he was mistaken they were bright now with tears. Her voice had a little break in it.

"It was a surprise I was preparing for Robert. His birthday is next month. I knew he wanted a new gun and you know I'm dreadfully stupid about sporting things. I wanted to talk to Geoff. about it. I thought I'd get him to order it for me."

"Perhaps the terms of the letter are not very clear to your recollection.

36

Will you have another look at it."

"No, I don't want to," she said quickly.

"Does it seem to you the sort of letter a woman would write to a somewhat distant acquaintance because she wanted to consult him about buying a gun?"

"I daresay it's rather extravagant and emotional. I do express myself like that, you know. I'm quite prepared to admit it's very silly." She smiled. "And after all, Geoff. Hammond wasn't quite a distant acquaintance. When he was ill I'd nursed him like a mother. I asked him to come when Robert was away, because Robert wouldn't have him in the house."

Mr. Joyce was tired of sitting so long in the same position. He rose and walked once or twice up and down the room, choosing the words he proposed to say; then he leaned over the back of the chair in which he had been sitting. He spoke slowly in a tone of deep gravity.

"Mrs. Crosbie, I want to talk to you very, very seriously. This case was comparatively plain sailing. There was only one point which seemed to me to require explanation: as far as I could judge, you had fired no less than four shots into Hammond when he was lying on the ground. It was hard to accept the possibility that a delicate, frightened, and habitually self-controlled woman, of gentle nature and refined instincts, should have surrendered to an absolutely uncontrolled frenzy. But of course it was admissible. Although Geoffrey Hammond was much liked and on the whole thought highly of, I was prepared to prove that he was the sort of man who might be guilty of the crime which in justification of your act you accused him of. The fact, which was discovered after his death, that he had been living with a Chinese woman gave us something very definite to go upon. That robbed him of any sympathy which might have been left for him. We made up our minds to make use of the odium which such a connection cast upon him in the minds of all respectable people. I told your husband this morning that I was certain of an acquittal, and I wasn't just telling him that to give him heart. I do not believe the assessors would have left the court."

They looked into one another's eyes. Mrs. Crosbie was strangely still. She was like a little bird paralysed by the fascination of a snake. He went on in the same quiet tones.

"But this letter has thrown an entirely different complexion on the case. I am your legal adviser, I shall represent you in Court. I take your story as you tell it me, and I shall conduct your defence according to its terms. It may be that I believe your statements, and it may be that I doubt them. The duty of counsel is to persuade the Court that the evidence placed before it is not such as to justify it in bringing in a verdict of guilty, and any private opinion he may have of the guilt or innocence of his client is entirely beside the point."

He was astonished to see in Leslie's eyes the flicker of a smile. Piqued, he went on somewhat dryly.

"You're not going to deny that Hammond came to your house at your urgent, and I may even say, hysterical invitation?"

Mrs. Crosbie, hesitating for an instant, seemed to consider.

"They can prove that the letter was taken to his bungalow by one of the house-boys. He rode over on his bicycle."

"You mustn't expect other people to be stupider than you. The letter will put them on the track of suspicions which have entered nobody's head. I will not tell you what I personally thought when I saw the copy. I do not wish you to tell me anything but what is needed to save your neck."

Mrs. Crosbie gave a shrill cry. She sprang to her feet, white with terror.

"You don't think they'd hang me?"

"If they came to the conclusion that you hadn't killed Hammond in self-defence, it would be the duty of the assessors to bring in a verdict of guilty. The charge is murder. It would be the duty of the judge to sentence you to death."

"But what can they prove?" she gasped.

"I don't know what they can prove. You know. I don't want to know. But if their suspicions are aroused, if they begin to make inquiries, if the natives are questioned — what is it that can be discovered?"

She crumpled up suddenly. She fell on the floor before he could catch her. She had fainted. He looked round the room for water, but there was none there, and he did not want to be disturbed. He stretched her out on the floor, and kneeling beside her waited for her to recover. When she opened her eyes he was disconcerted by the ghastly fear that he saw in them.

"Keep quite still," he said. "You'll be better in a moment."

"You won't let them hang me," she whispered.

She began to cry, hysterically, while in undertones he sought to quieten her.

"For goodness sake pull yourself together," he said.

"Give me a minute."

Her courage was amazing. He could see the effort she made to regain her self-control, and soon she was once more calm.

"Let me get up now."

He gave her his hand and helped her to her feet. Taking her arm, he led her to the chair. She sat down wearily.

"Don't talk to me for a minute or two," she said.

"Very well."

When at last she spoke it was to say something which he did not expect. She gave a little sigh.

"I'm afraid I've made rather a mess of things," she said.

He did not answer, and once more there was a silence.

"Isn't it possible to get hold of the letter?" she said at last.

"I do not think anything would have been said to me about it, if the person in whose possession it is was not prepared to sell it."

"Who's got it?"

"The Chinese woman who was living in Hammond's house."

A spot of colour flickered for an instant on Leslie's cheek-bones.

"Does she want an awful lot for it?"

"I imagine that she has a very shrewd idea of its value. I doubt if it would be possible to get hold of it except for a very large sum."

"Are you going to let me be hanged?"

"Do you think it's so simple as all that to secure possession of an unwelcome piece of evidence? It's no different from suborning a witness. You have no right to make any such suggestion to me."

"Then what is going to happen to me?"

"Justice must take its course."

She grew very pale. A little shudder passed through her body.

"I put myself in your hands. Of course I have no right to ask you to do anything that isn't proper."

Mr. Joyce had not bargained for the little break in her voice which her habitual self-restraint made quite intolerably moving. She looked at him with humble eyes, and he thought that if he rejected their appeal they would haunt him for the rest of his life. After all, nothing could bring poor Hammond back to life again. He wondered what really was the explanation of that letter. It was not fair to conclude from it that she had killed Hammond without provocation. He had lived in the East a long time and his sense of professional honour was not perhaps so acute as it had been twenty years before. He stared at the floor. He made up his mind to do something which he knew was unjustifiable, but it stuck in his throat and he felt dully resentful towards Leslie. It embarrassed him a little to speak.

"I don't know exactly what your husband's circumstances are?"

Flushing a rosy red, she shot a swift glance at him.

"He has a good many tin shares and a small share in two or three rubber estates. I suppose he could raise money."

"He would have to be told what it was for."

She was silent for a moment. She seemed to think.

"He's in love with me still. He would make any sacrifice to save me. Is there any need for him to see the letter?"

Mr. Joyce frowned a little, and, quick to notice, she went on.

"Robert is an old friend of yours. I'm not asking you to do anything for me, I'm asking you to save a rather simple, kind man who never did you any harm from all the pain that's possible."

Mr. Joyce did not reply. He rose to go and Mrs. Crosbie, with the grace that was natural to her, held out her hand. She was shaken by the scene, and her look was haggard, but she made a brave attempt to speed him with courtesy.

"It's so good of you to take all this trouble for me. I can't begin to tell you how grateful I am."

Mr. Joyce returned to his office. He sat in his own room, quite still, attempting to do no work, and pondered. His imagination brought him many strange ideas. He shuddered a little. At last there was the discreet knock on the door which he was expecting. Ong Chi Seng came in.

"I was just going out to have my tiffin, sir," he said.

"All right."

"I didn't know if there was anything you wanted before I went, sir."

"I don't think so. Did you make another appointment for Mr. Reed?"

"Yes, sir. He will come at three o'clock."

"Good."

Ong Chi Seng turned away, walked to the door, and put his long slim fingers on the handle. Then, as though on an afterthought, he turned back.

"Is there anything you wish me to say to my friend, sir?"

Although Ong Chi Seng spoke English so admirably he had still a difficulty with the letter R, and he pronounced it 'fliend'.

"What friend?"

"About the letter Mrs. Crosbie wrote to Hammond deceased, sir."

"Oh! I'd forgotten about that. I mentioned it to Mrs. Crosbie and she denies having written anything of the sort. It's evidently a forgery."

Mr. Joyce took the copy from his pocket and handed it to Ong Chi Seng. Ong Chi Seng ignored the gesture.

"In that case, sir, I suppose there would be no objection if my fliend delivered the letter to the Deputy Public Prosecutor."

"None. But I don't quite see what good that would do your friend."

"My fliend, sir, thought it was his duty in the interests of justice."

"I am the last man in the world to interfere with anyone who wishes

41

to do his duty, Chi Seng."

The eyes of the lawyer and of the Chinese clerk met. Not the shadow of a smile hovered on the lips of either, but they understood each other perfectly.

"I quite understand, sir," said Ong Chi Seng, "but from my study of the case R.*v*. Crosbie I am of opinion that the production of such a letter would be damaging to our client."

"I have always had a very high opinion of your legal acumen, Chi Seng."

"It has occured to me, sir, that if I could persuade my fliend to induce the Chinese woman who has the letter to deliver it into our hands it would save a great deal of trouble."

Mr. Joyce idly drew faces on his blotting-paper.

"I suppose your friend is a business man. In what circumstances do you think he would be induced to part with the letter?"

"He has not got the letter. The Chinese woman has the letter. He is only a relation of the Chinese woman. She is an ignorant woman; she did not know the value of that letter till my fliend told her."

"What value did he put on it?"

"Ten thousand dollars, sir."

"Good God! Where on earth do you suppose Mrs. Crosbie can get ten thousand dollars! I tell you the letter's a forgery."

He looked up at Ong Chi Seng as he spoke. The clerk was unmoved by the outburst. He stood at the side of the desk, civil, cool and observant.

"Mr. Crosbie owns an eighth share of the Betong Rubber Estate and a sixth share of the Selantan River Rubber Estate. I have a fliend who will lend him the money on the security of his property."

"You have a large circle of acquaintance, Chi Seng."

"Yes, sir."

"Well, you can tell them all to go to hell. I would never advise Mr. Crosbie to give a penny more than five thousand for a letter that can be very easily explained."

"The Chinese woman does not want to sell the letter, sir. My fliend took a long time to persuade her. It is useless to offer her less than the sum mentioned."

Mr. Joyce looked at Ong Chi Seng for at least three minutes. The clerk bore the searching scrutiny without embarrassment. He stood in a respectful attitude with downcast eyes. Mr. Joyce knew his man. Clever fellow, Chi Seng, he thought, I wonder how much he's going to get out of it.

"Ten thousand dollars is a very large sum."

"Mr. Crosbie will certainly pay it rather than see his wife hanged, sir."

Again Mr. Joyce paused. What more did Chi Seng know than he had said? He must be pretty sure of his ground if he was obviously so unwilling to bargain. That sum had been fixed because whoever it was that was managing the affair knew it was the largest amount that Robert Crosbie could raise.

"Where is the Chinese woman now?" asked Mr. Joyce.

"She is staying at the house of my fliend, sir."

"Will she come here?"

"I think it more better if you go to her, sir. I can take you to the house to-night and she will give you the letter. She is a very ignorant woman, sir, and she does not understand cheques."

"I wasn't thinking of giving her a cheque. I will bring banknotes with me."

"It would only be waste of valuable time to bring less than ten thousand dollars, sir."

"I quite understand."

"I will go and tell my fliend after I have had my tiffin, sir."

"Very good. You'd better meet me outside the club at ten o'clock to-night."

"With pleasure, sir," said Ong Chi Seng.

He gave Mr. Joyce a little bow and left the room. Mr. Joyce went out to have luncheon, too. He went to the club and here, as he had expected, he saw Robert Crosbie. He was sitting at a crowded table, and as he passed him, looking for a place, Mr. Joyce touched him on the shoulder.

"I'd like a word or two with you before you go," he said.

"Right you are. Let me know when you're ready."

Mr. Joyce had made up his mind how to tackle him. He played a rubber of bridge after luncheon in order to allow time for the club to empty itself. He did not want on this particular matter to see Crosbie in his office. Presently Crosbie came into the card-room and looked on till the game was finished. The other players went on their various affairs, and the two were left alone.

"A rather unfortunate thing has happened, old man," said Mr. Joyce, in a tone which he sought to render as casual as possible. "It appears that your wife sent a letter to Hammond asking him to come to the bungalow on the night he was killed."

"But that's impossible," cried Crosbie. "She's always stated that she had had no communication with Hammond. I know from my own knowledge that she hadn't set eyes on him for a couple of months."

"The fact remains that the letter exists. It's in the possession of the Chinese woman Hammond was living with. Your wife meant to give you a present on your birthday, and she wanted Hammond to help her to get it. In the emotional excitement that she suffered from after the tragedy, she forgot all about it, and having once denied having any communication with Hammond she was afraid to say that she had made a mistake. It was, of course, very unfortunate, but I daresay it was not unnatural."

Crosbie did not speak. His large, red face bore an expression of complete bewilderment, and Mr. Joyce was at once relieved and exasperated by his lack of comprehension. He was a stupid man, and Mr. Joyce had no patience with stupidity. But his distress since the catastrophe had touched a soft spot in the lawyer's heart; and Mrs. Crosbie had struck the right note when she asked him to help her, not for her sake, but for her husband's.

"I need not tell you that it would be very awkward if this letter found its way into the hands of the prosecution. Your wife has lied, and she would be asked to explain the lie. It alters things a little if Hammond did not intrude, an unwanted guest, but came to your house by invitation. It would be easy to arouse in the assessors a certain indecision of mind."

Mr. Joyce hesitated. He was face to face now with his decision. If it had been a time for humour, he could have smiled at the reflection that he was taking so grave a step and that the man for whom he was taking it had not the smallest conception of its gravity. If he gave the matter a thought, he probably imagined that what Mr. Joyce was doing was what any lawyer did in the ordinary run of business.

"My dear Robert, you are not only my client, but my friend. I think we must get hold of that letter. It'll cost a good deal of money. Except for that I should have preferred to say nothing to you about it."

"How much?"

"Ten thousand dollars."

"That's a devil of a lot. With the slump and one thing and another it'll take just about all I've got."

"Can you get it at once?"

"I suppose so. Old Charlie Meadows will let me have it on my tin shares and on those two estates I'm interested in."

"Then will you?"

"Is it absolutely necessary?"

"If you want your wife to be acquitted."

Crosbie grew very red. His mouth sagged strangely.

"But ..." he could not find words, his face now was purple. "But I don't understand. She can explain. You don't mean to say they'd find her guilty? They couldn't hang her for putting a noxious vermin out of the way."

"Of course they wouldn't hang her. They might only find her guilty of manslaughter. She'd probably get off with two or three years."

Crosbie started to his feet and his red face was distraught with horror.

"Three years."

Then something seemed to dawn in that slow intelligence of his. His mind was darkness across which shot suddenly a flash of lightning, and though the succeeding darkness was as profound, there remained the memory of something not seen but perhaps just described. Mr. Joyce saw that Crosbie's big red hands, coarse and hard with all the odd jobs he had set them to, trembled.

"What was the present she wanted to make me?"

"She says she wanted to give you a new gun."

Once more that great red face flushed a deeper red.

"When have you got to have the money ready?"

There was something old in his voice now. It sounded as though he spoke with invisible hands clutching at this throat.

"At ten o'clock to-night. I thought you could bring it to my office at about six."

"Is the woman coming to you?"

"No, I'm going to her."

"I'll bring the money. I'll come with you."

Mr. Joyce looked at him sharply.

"Do you think there's any need for you to do that? I think it would be better if you left me to deal with this matter by myself."

"It's my money, isn't it? I'm going to come."

Mr. Joyce shrugged his shoulders. They rose and shook hands. Mr. Joyce looked at him curiously.

At ten o'clock they met in the empty club.

"Everything all right?" asked Mr. Joyce.

"Yes, I've got the money in my pocket."

"Let's go then."

They walked down the steps. Mr. Joyce's car was waiting for them in the square, silent at that hour, and as they came to it Ong Chi Seng stepped out of the shadow of a house. He took his seat beside the driver and gave him a direction. They drove past the Hotel de l'Europe and turned up by the Sailor's Home to get into Victoria Street. Here the

Chinese shops were still open, idlers lounged about, and in the roadway rickshaws and motor-cars and gharries gave a busy air to the scene. Suddenly their car stopped and Chi Seng turned round.

"I think it more better if we walk here, sir," he said.

They got out and he went on. They followed a step or two behind. Then he asked them to stop.

"You wait here, sir. I go in and speak to my fliend."

He went into a shop, open to the street, where three or four Chinese were standing behind the counter. It was one of those strange shops where nothing was on view, and you wondered what it was they sold there. They saw him address a stout man in a duck suit with a large gold chain across his breast, and the man shot a quick glance out into the night. He gave Chi Seng a key and Chi Seng came out. He beckoned to the two men waiting and slid into a doorway at the side of the shop. They followed him and found themselves at the foot of a flight of stairs.

"If you wait a minute I will light a match," he said, always resourceful. "You come upstairs, please."

He held a Japanese match in front of them, but it scarcely dispelled the darkness and they groped their way up behind him. On the first floor he unlocked a door and going in lit a gas-jet.

"Come in, please," he said.

It was a small square room, with one window, and the only furniture consisted of two low Chinese beds covered with matting. In one corner was a large chest, with an elaborate lock, and on this stood a shabby tray with an opium pipe on it and a lamp. There was in the room the faint, acrid scent of the drug. They sat down and Ong Chi Seng offered them cigarettes. In a moment the door was opened by the fat Chinaman whom they had seen behind the counter. He bade them good-evening in very good English, and sat down by the side of his fellow-countryman.

"The Chinese woman is just coming," said Chi Seng.

A boy from the shop brought in a tray with a teapot and cups and the Chinaman offered them a cup of tea. Crosbie refused. The Chinese talked to one another in undertones, but Crosbie and Mr. Joyce were silent. At last there was the sound of a voice outside; someone was calling in a low tone; and the Chinaman went to the door. He opened it, spoke a few words, and ushered a woman in. Mr. Joyce looked at her. He had heard much about her since Hammond's death, but he had never seen her. She was a stoutish person, not very young, with a broad, phlegmatic face, she was powdered and rouged and her eyebrows were a thin black line, but she gave you the impression of a woman of character. She wore a pale blue jacket and a white skirt, her costume was not quite European nor quite Chinese, but on her feet were little Chinese silk slippers. She wore heavy gold chains round her neck, gold bangles on her wrists, gold ear-rings, and elaborate gold pins in her black hair. She walked in slowly, with the air of a woman sure of herself, but with a certain heaviness of tread, and sat down on the bed beside Ong Chi Seng. He said something to her and nodding she gave an incurious glance at the two white men.

"Has she got the letter?" asked Mr. Joyce.

"Yes, sir."

Crosbie said nothing, but produced a roll of five hundred-dollar notes. He counted out twenty and handed them to Chi Seng.

"Will you see if that is correct?"

The clerk counted them and gave them to the fat Chinaman.

"Quite correct, sir."

The Chinaman counted them once more and put them in his pocket. He spoke again to the woman and she drew from her bosom a letter. She gave it to Chi Seng who cast his eyes over it.

"This is the right document, sir," he said, and was about to give it to Mr. Joyce when Crosbie took it from him.

"Let me look at it," he said.

Mr. Joyce watched him read and then held out his hand for it.

"You'd better let me have it."

Crosbie folded it up deliberately and put it in his pocket.

"No, I'm going to keep it myself. It's cost me enough money."

Mr. Joyce made no rejoinder. The three Chinese watched the little passage, but what they thought about it, or whether they thought, it was impossible to tell from their impassive countenances. Mr. Joyce rose to his feet.

"Do you want me any more to-night, sir?" said Ong Chi Seng.

"No." He knew that the clerk wished to stay behind in order to get his agreed share of the money, and he turned to Crosbie. "Are you ready?"

Crosbie did not answer, but stood up. The Chinaman went to the door and opened it for them. Chi Seng found a bit of candle and lit it in order to light them down, and the two Chinese accompanied them to the street. They left the woman sitting quietly on the bed smoking a cigarette. When they reached the street the Chinese left them and went once more upstairs.

"What are you going to do with that letter?" asked Mr. Joyce.

"Keep it."

They walked to where the car was waiting for them and here Mr. Joyce offered his friend a lift. Crosbie shook his head.

"I'm going to walk." He hesitated a little and shuffled his feet. "I went to Singapore on the night of Hammond's death partly to buy a new gun that a man I knew wanted to dispose of. Good-night."

He disappeared quickly into the darkness.

Mr. Joyce was quite right about the trial. The assessors went into court fully determined to acquit Mrs. Crosbie. She gave evidence on her own behalf. She told her story simply and with straightforwardness. The D.P.P. was a kindly man and it was plain that he took no great pleasure in his task. He asked the necessary questions in a deprecating manner. His speech for the prosecution might really have been a speech for the defence, and the assessors took less than five minutes to consider their popular verdict. It was impossible to prevent the great outburst of applause with which it was received by the crowd that packed the court house. The judge congratulated Mrs. Crosbie and she was a free woman.

No one had expressed a more violent disapprobation of Hammond's behaviour than Mrs. Joyce; she was a woman loyal to her friends and she had insisted on the Crosbie's staying with her after the trial, for she in common with everyone else had no doubt of the result, till they could make arrangements to go away. It was out of the question for poor, dear, brave Leslie to return to the bungalow at which the horrible catastrophe had taken place. The trial was over by half-past twelve and when they reached the Joyce's house a grand luncheon was awaiting them. Cocktails were ready, Mrs. Joyce's million dollar cocktail was celebrated through all the Malay States, and Mrs. Joyce drank to Leslie's health. She was a talkative, vivacious woman, and now she was in the highest spirits. It was fortunate, for the rest of them were silent. She did not wonder, her husband never had much to say, and the other two were naturally exhausted from the long strain to which they had been subjected. During luncheon she carried on a bright and spirited monologue. Then coffee was served.

"Now, children," she said in her gay, bustling fashion, "you must have a rest and after tea I shall take you both for a drive to the sea."

Mr. Joyce, who lunched at home only by exception, had of course to go back to his office.

"I'm afraid I can't do that, Mrs. Joyce," said Crosbie. "I've got to get back to the estate at once."

"Not to-day?" she cried.

"Yes, now. I've neglected it for too long and I have urgent business. But I shall be very grateful if you will keep Leslie until we have decided what to do."

Mrs. Joyce was about to expostulate, but her husband prevented her.

"If he must go, he must, and there's an end of it."

There was something in the lawyer's tone which made her look at him quickly. She held her tongue and there was a moment's silence. Then Crosbie spoke again.

"If you'll forgive me, I'll start at once so that I can get there before dark." He rose from the table. "Will you come and see me off, Leslie!"

"Of course."

They went out of the dining-room together.

"I think that's rather inconsiderate of him," said Mrs. Joyce. "He must know that Leslie wants to be with him just now."

"I'm sure he wouldn't go if it wasn't absolutely necessary."

"Well, I'll just see that Leslie's room is ready for her. She wants a complete rest, of course, and then amusement."

Mrs. Joyce left the room and Joyce sat down again. In a short time he heard Crosbie start the engine of his motor-cycle and then noisily scrunch over the gravel of the garden path. He got up and went into the drawing-room. Mrs. Crosbie was standing in the middle of it, looking into space, and in her hand was an open letter. He recognised it. She gave him a glance as he came in and he saw that she was deathly pale.

"He knows," she whispered.

Mr. Joyce went up to her and took the letter from her hand. He lit a match and set the paper afire. She watched it burn. When he could hold it no longer he dropped it on the tiled floor and they both looked at the paper curl and blacken. Then he trod it into ashes with his foot.

"What does he know?"

She gave him a long, long stare and into her eyes came a strange look. Was it contempt or despair? Mr. Joyce could not tell.

"He knows that Geoff. was my lover."

Mr. Joyce made no movement and uttered no sound.

"He'd been my lover for years. He became my lover almost immediately after he came back from the war. We knew how careful we must be. When we became lovers I pretended I was tired of him, and he seldom came to the house when Robert was there. I used to drive out to a place we knew and he met me, two or three times a week, and when Robert went to Singapore he used to come to the bungalow late, when the boys had gone for the night. We saw one another constantly, all the time, and not a soul had the smallest suspicion of it. And then lately, a year ago, he began to change. I didn't know what was the matter. I couldn't believe that he didn't care for me any more. He always denied it. I was frantic. I made him scenes. Sometimes I thought he hated me. Oh, if you knew what agonies I endured. I passed through hell. I knew he didn't want me any more and I wouldn't let him go. Misery! Misery! I loved him. I'd given him everything. He was all my life. And then I heard he was living with a Chinese woman. I couldn't believe it. I wouldn't believe it. At last I saw her, I saw her with my own eyes, walking in the village, with her gold bracelets and her necklaces, an old, fat, Chinese woman. She was older than I was. Horrible! They all knew in the kampong that she was his mistress. And when I passed her, she looked at me and I knew that she knew I was his mistress too. I sent for him. I told him I must see him. You've read the letter. I was mad to write it. I didn't know what I was doing. I didn't care. I hadn't seen him for ten days. It was a lifetime. And when last we'd parted he took me in his arms and kissed me, and told me not to worry. And he went straight from my arms to hers."

She had been speaking in a low voice, vehemently, and now she stopped and wrung her hands.

"That damned letter. We'd always been so careful. He always tore up any word I wrote to him the moment he'd read it. How was I to know he'd leave that one? He came, and I told him I knew about the Chinawoman. He denied it. He said it was only scandal. I was beside myself. I don't know what I said to him. Oh, I hated him then. I tore him limb from limb. I said everything I could to wound him. I insulted him. I could have spat in his face. And at last he turned on me. He told me he was sick and tired of me and never wanted to see me again. He said I bored him to death. And then he acknowledged that it was true about the Chinawoman. He said he'd known her for years, before the war, and she was the only woman who really meant anything to him, and the rest was just pastime. And he said he was glad I knew, and now at last I'd leave him alone. And then I don't know what happened, I was beside myself, I saw red. I seized the revolver and I fired. He gave a cry and I saw I'd hit him. He staggered and rushed for the verandah. I ran after him and fired again. He fell, and then I stood over him and I fired and fired till the revolver went click, click, and I knew there were no more cartridges."

At last she stopped, panting. Her face was no longer human, it was distorted with cruelty, and rage and pain. You would never have thought that this quiet, refined woman was capable of such fiendish passion. Mr. Joyce took a step backwards. He was absolutely aghast at the sight of her. It was not a face, it was a gibbering, hideous mask. Then they heard a voice calling from another room, a loud, friendly, cheerful voice. It was Mrs. Joyce.

"Come along, Leslie darling, your room's ready. You must be dropping with sleep."

Mrs. Crosbie's features gradually composed themselves. Those passions, so clearly delineated, were smoothed away as with your hand you would smooth a crumpled paper, and in a minute the face was cool and calm and unlined. She was a trifle pale, but her lips broke into a pleasant, affable smile. She was once more the well-bred and even distinguished woman.

"I'm coming, Dorothy dear. I'm sorry to give you so much trouble."

TIDA APA
(No Matter)

In this land of dust and heat
  There's a phrase so nice and neat
You hear it everywhere you go
  In places high, in places low
  'Tis always "Tida Apa."

The Malay man works hard all day
  He doesn't earn a decent pay
"Kerja pagi, makan malam"
  So long as he can fill his "dalam"
  He murmurs "Tida Apa."

On the race course I was bitten
  But with remorse am I now smitten?
Not on your life—this cheerful phrase
  Adds lustre to the dullest days
  I just say "Tida Apa."

I made a careless deal in rubber
  I'm hit so hard I'd like to blubber
But do I weep now?—No, not I!
  I say with a regretful sigh
  Oh "Tida Apa."

When I'm dead and in my grave
  This the epitaph I crave
"Ini orang suda mati
  Banya orang susa hati
  Tapi 'Tida Apa'."

IN BED WITH A DUTCH WIFE
by Hugh Wilkinson

DE BOSCO is at present trying to kill the mosquitoes, which have got inside the curtains round his bed; he says there are so many inside, that it would be far less trouble to "shut them in" and sleep on the sofa! They seem to make straight for the curtains, in which they either discover or eat a little hole, through which they then swarm, and, taking up their various positions inside, cheerfully and patiently wait for their victim. The temperature in the room is now (11 p.m.) only 82°, but it is a moist heat which makes it unpleasant. There are several lizards on the walls of the room: they are harmless little creatures to everything but flies and other insects, which they stalk and pounce upon in the most wonderful way. Last night we had a deluge of rain, and today two tremendous tropical showers; it rains here without exception nearly every day, and it is nearly the same climate and temperature the whole year round, and days and nights are of equal length. It is very steamy and hot, making one feel flabby and limp, and not giving one's clothes a chance of drying day or night. Some Frenchman somewhere says, that this tropical heat is so great that clothes of any sort are insupportable. "I make von bundle of dem, upon which I seat myself, and in a short time they are wringing wet." In the hotels about these melting regions, what is called a "Dutch wife" is always provided for one's nightly comfort. Don't be alarmed, it isn't what you are thinking of. My bedfellow and I very soon quarrelled, and, after a short but stormy acquaintance, I remained sole partner of the bed. A "Dutch wife" is an elongated bolster which one places between one's two ankles and one's wrists for as much coolness as is possible; but if mine had been alive she couldn't have been more worrying. She seemed to be most awfully in the way, and as I could get no peace with her in bed, and as she was rapidly getting me out of it, I thought it better to bring matters to a crisis by a tussle and stand-up fight, which was ended in my favour by a vigorous kick, which sent her bang through the mosquito-curtains to the other side of the room. This was my first, and will be my last, experience of a Dutch wife. The same thing went on in the other room to the war-cry of "Bachelorhood or death." Talking of Dutch wives reminds me that we haven't had any butter since we left Europe. We would give almost the price of a king's ransom for some good brown bread and Devonshire butter. We had once or twice in India butter made from buffalo milk, but didn't care much for it; we could easily do without it, and after the first trial did so. The stuff on the *Ceylon* is like half-melted train oil.

For vegetation, winter and summer are the same; when the leaves think they have been on long enough they fall off; and when fruit takes it into its head to appear and ripen, it does so....

Yesterday we inspected the markets, which were very interesting, the fish-market especially so, with all its quaint and many-coloured fish. There were the usual very large prawns, eight or ten inches long, and a thin misshapen-fish which looked for all the world like the tin fish at a pantomime at home; another fish, just like an old maid we have in our county, and quite as good-looking in the face; you have seen the fish in the Aquaria at home, nearly round, and about the size and shape of a football. We also saw many cuttle-fish, and little fish like whitebait; immense cockles, some very repulsive-looking king crabs, and some small black ones; a quantity of sea-snails of a most brilliant red colour, and very lively. Nothing new to us in the fruit-market. We are told that neither the mangosteen nor durian are yet ripe; of course we are very much distressed at this, but we have oranges, bananas and pineapples to console ourselves with. Amongst the vegetables there are many we have never seen before, but recognise a great many, including lettuces, onions, tomatoes, sweet potatoes, and the bright scarlet chillies. The oranges all about these regions never change the colour of their skins, which are the same bright green colour, even when perfectly ripe.

The Chinamen, who are far superior to the other brown races here, are quietly elbowing them out of everything; they seem to be ubiquitous. It is so strange to see them at their grub, with their little basins close to their mouths in one hand, and their chopsticks, which they so daintily and cleverly use, in the other. All the servants in the hotel are Chinamen, and half a dozen of them have come into our rooms this morning on the pretence of doing one thing or another. They are all cast in the same mould, and are consequently exactly alike. We are only able to tell it isn't the same fellow by the slight diversity in his dress, and knowing that the same person would not be such a fool as to keep coming in half a dozen times to do what he might have done at once. The Chinaman is spoken of as being the best of servants, and is always addressed "boy".

We went to a Malay theatre in the evening, but it was so stupid and incomprehensible to us that we went to another one, a Hindu theatre, which was quite as bad, everything being to us so absolutely without any meaning, that they appeared to be a pack of lunatics....

This afternoon we leave for Johore, the Maharajah having most kindly invited the passengers to a banquet, and afterwards to a ball, and to spend the following day there before leaving for Manila.

from Sunny Lands and Seas (1883)

AN OLD TRAVELLER AT RAFFLES
by C. D. Mckellers

SINGAPORE ways were new to me, though those who have dwelt in the East will scorn my ignorance. My bedroom opened on the long, wide balcony, and the space in front, partly enclosed and furnished with table and chairs, was my sitting-room. The little swing-door of the bedroom reached neither floor nor ceiling, so that it concealed little of the room. There were two dressing-rooms and one of these was my bathroom. It also had a little swing-door opening into the inner hall. Chinese "boys," as they are called, passed to and fro, in and out, regardless of me or my state of apparel. They paid no attention to anything I said, nor could I bar them out anyway. When I wanted them I had to go and call them, and it so happened that I wanted many things, for I was discarding all my garments worn on the voyage, so that no New Guinea fever microbes should abide with me, and what did on the ship would not do in smart Singapore. After many appeals to passing servants, a languid Englishman in the next balcony compartment said to me, "Excuse me, but these are my boys you are ordering about." I apologised and asked how I could possibly know that, as they seemed to use my room as a passage. He said they were incorrigible that way, and explained that here one engaged at once one's own Chinese boys to wait on one — they were not hotel servants at all! He sent for a hotel servant for me for the meanwhile.

But now I am getting into the way of things here. I could not get on without attention, so said to the hotel people I must have boys to wait on me, and to "put them in the bill." Now I appear to have six. They all look the same and I no longer lack attention or attendance. I live a life of mingled laziness and overpowering energy, half in my chair here and half tearing about Singapore in "rickshaws." My neighbour next door I do not see unless I advance to the front of the balcony. He then takes his cigar out of his mouth and says "Ah!" He is always in his chair in exactly the same attitude with apparently the same cigar at the same stage. He never smiles and seldom speaks. Once as I was leaving the hotel my conscience pricked me and I thought perhaps he was ill and needed sympathy, so I returned the length of the huge building and along the balcony.

"Are you ill — are you well — are you all right?" I asked.

He looked astonished, then said, "All right."

"That's all right," I said, and departed, feeling satisfied and quite unable to prolong this interesting conversation. I have since discovered his vocabulary is limited to "Ah!" "Yes and No," "Pretty well," "Not bad," and "All right." It simplifies life.

A suspicion has just dawned on me that two of my attendants are his — they seem familiar somehow. But I don't know where any of them come from — if they are hotel servants, or his, or mine, or whose. I just accept the situation — it suits the climate. Anyway, already they are by way of "taking care of me," and grinning faces — all the same — and flying pigtails are everywhere.

My programme is, after my morning tub, to go and lie in my pyjamas with bare feet in my long chair. My tea is there, fruit, smoking material, books, and a Singapore newspaper. If I want anything I pull the nearest passing bell-rope — I mean pigtail — and point at something. They are wonderful, though; they know now even without my pointing. I notice, too, they have suddenly coiled their pigtails in an elegant coronet round their heads. I wonder why? I never see any one attending to my neighbour next door, but I can't help that. All my baggage is unpacked, strewn about, and in process of repair and cleaning. They did it all unasked, so I don't worry.

The first night I got into a rickshaw, and said I must be driven — or whatever you say in a rickshaw — very quickly all round the town. We tore along, scattering every one right and left; went first through a crowded street, and I had visions of painted ladies rising in balconies and rows of Japanese girls calling out in chorus, but we tore past unheeding and raced all over the place. "Here — hi!" I cried at last; "not so fast — stop!" whereupon my coolie came to a dead stop and nearly threw me out. I admire much the fat, rich-looking Chinese driving about in grand carriages with liveried Malay servants on the box, and I saw three stout Chinamen packed into one rickshaw, and their coolie nearly fainting with the weight. These Chinese become rich and prosperous under our Government, but if they went to China would lose their wealth and their heads — but it will not be always so.

from Scented Isles and Coral Gardens (1912)

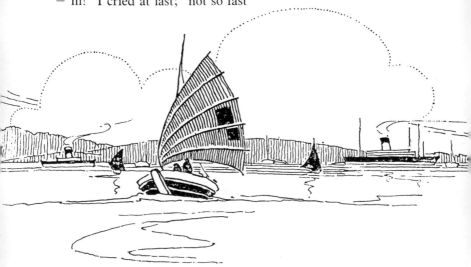

60

WHAT'S IN A NAME?

ON the principle of the derivation of certain English names, such as Smith, Cooper, Fowler, etc. from the trade or calling of the early members of the family, the Author, as a result of profound research, ventures to suggest the following origins of local interest:—

Ah Mee
The rubber broker.

Eu Goh
The man who heard a burglar and sent his wife to investigate.

So Lo Meow
The minstrel.

Hup Wee Goh
The lift attendant.

Wan Sum Wong
The man who backed every loser.

Chin Hup
The barber.

Chew Hup
The betel-nut merchant.

Bee Seck
The medicine man.

See Seck
The sampan man.

Soon Eu See
The optician.

Ay-am, ay-am!
Are yer?
Ay-am, ay-am!!
Well, wot the 'ell are yer?

Lock Hup
The warder.

Tee Aw Gan
The dentist.

Wu Hing
The suitor.

Jin He Sing
The bar-boy.

Hee Lye Ying
The fortune teller.

Wee Fit Eu
The tailor.

Onn Lee Mee
The bullock-cart driver who wants ALL the road.

Tan Kew Tuan
The beggar.

THAT FIRST TOPEE.

We have often noticed the affection evince

THAT FIRST TOPEE.

by the new-comer, for his first topee.

OLD BUGIS STREET
by F. D. Ommanney

THERE are miles of these streets and of crowded, noisy alleyways, all very much the same, flanked by vertical signboards bearing Chinese characters and roofed with intimate laundry. They are filled with shouting, swarming life far into the night. Many are lined with food stalls under canvas awnings, lit by paraffin lamps. The Chinese largely eat in the street. There squat the thin men in striped pyjama trousers and singlets, perched on stools like hungry emaciated birds, their feet on the top of the stool and their angular buttocks suspended in space. They hold their rice bowls up to their mouths and scoop the rice in with a shovelling motion of the chopsticks. Or the chopsticks peck into the bowls like beaks.

At the eating stalls the food is stewed in huge copper pans over charcoal braziers. Clouds of steam obscure the lights and an utterly delicious smell fills the air. The food itself is displayed under the awnings in brightly coloured piles and festoons. Its appearance is perhaps slightly less appetizing than its smell, for, in addition to the dried, flattened cuttle-fish, the trussed and naked poultry, the piles of noodles, cockles and eggs, there hangs from hooks every known form of guts, innards, offal and lights. Perhaps because they have a history punctuated by famines and by scarcities due to wars, natural disasters and pestilences, the Chinese seem to have learnt to eat practically anything, and no part or organ is too inconsiderable. All are equally but variously delicious when cooked. Here, glistening coldly in the lamplight, are veils of tripe, slabs of liver, ropes of intestines, pancreases, spleens and kidneys. Under the brilliant lights at each stall, surrounded by auras of rising steam, accomplished cooks work deftly and with intense concentration, basting chickens, tossing noodles, adding a little of this, a pinch of that, chopping, pounding, stirring. And along the main road at the end of the street the traffic roars by and the crowd idly saunters and changes endlessly.

A short thoroughfare such as this, filled with eating stalls, connects two busy main roads. It is called Bugis Street after the early Malay pirates who frequented the islands across the Strait and made raids on Singapore before the British came. In this short street, a channel of light and noise, there are tables where you may sit and watch the ever-shifting pattern of life in Singapore. Waiters, in white singlets and shorts, run between the tables shouting orders over their customers' heads in a high-pitched sing-song chant. You may sit and drink here, if you wish, until the early hours of the morning, but about four o'clock they begin putting the tables away and the lights go out one by one. There will always be a taxi or a trishaw driver to take you home, or somewhere.

During the early part of the evening the customers at the tables are almost all Chinese. Many large family parties arrive with their numerous children. They choose one of the many circular tables and take a long time deciding what they will have. They eat with great gusto, all helping themselves with chopsticks from a dish or dishes in the middle of the table, dipping each morsel they pinch up with the chopsticks into little bowls containing sauce. Beggars drift to and fro with expressions of woe appropriate to their calling, pointing into their mouths and holding out tins for contributions. The customers, as a rule, take no notice of them. Later in the evening the Europeans begin to appear, the respectable and the not so respectable, the drunk and the sober, the quiet and the noisy. It is quite the thing, after a show or a party, to go down to Bugis Street. Men loosen their ties and women kick off their tight shoes under the table. The noisy get noisier and the drunk more drunk as the small hours after midnight draw on. The whores arrive, the same ones every night, and the beggars become more numerous and more insistent. I used to sit there and think that Bugis Street must be one of the most beautiful streets in the world in its own way, because of the lights and the ever-changing crowds and because of its irrepressible vitality. It is civilized because of its merciful, uncritical tolerance. Nothing matters, and the chief sins are not to smile and not to pay. All this is displeasing to authority, and many attempts have been made to do away with Bugis Street on one pretext or another, but somehow it survives. Perhaps these attempts have succeeded by now.

As I sit there and let time drift past like a river, a little girl, heavily made-up and looking many years older than her age, comes to my table and sings a song in a Chinese dialect. She has a slight, true, reedy little voice. Her eyes are never still for a moment and wander all over the tables as she sings. She never looks at the customer she is singing for. I give her twenty cents before she has got half-way through her song, which is the same every night, and she breaks off abruptly and runs away. This is Patsy, a pretty little thing with the very sharply slanted eyes and eyebrows which I love. They said she was being trained to be a whore, but she disappeared and Bugis Street knew her no more. Probably some Welfare Committee got hold of her and she is now being given a useless education and made to wear hideous clothes.

An old woman comes next with a child on her back. The boy is well able to walk, of course, and gives the show away by clamouring to be let down, kicking the old woman's sides with his legs as though spurring a horse. She found it profitable to carry him around thus four or five years ago when he was a tiny baby asleep on her back. Now he has become part of her stock-in-trade, a sort of stage property, but he has become so heavy that she has to lean forward to support his weight and his legs hang down on either side of her nearly to the ground.

Two children appear and place a screw of paper on my table. There are two metal bottle-tops inside it. It is a token which I am supposed to buy by giving them whatever I may think such a gift may be worth. It removes from the children the loss of face which outright begging would entail.

Little shoe-shine boys, organized in gangs, impish and *gamin*, little thugs in miniature, crawl under my chair and seize me by the ankles.

'Soo sine? Soo sine? Soo sine? Gimmy ten *sen*!'

I have to be fierce, otherwise they become a terrible nuisance.

SINGAPORE SLING

The girls, who have been sitting at tables together in the background for quite a long time, waiting for the street to fill up, now get up one by one as and when they think the moment appropriate, and saunter up and down in front of the tables so that everyone can see them. They all have English names which hide their true identity, and I do not suppose that any European knows what their true names are. Some are Chinese, some are Malays and some are evidently Eurasians. You can tell the Eurasian ones by their ladylike demeanour and because they love to tell you about their respectable white relations and forebears. Unfortunately they sometimes forget and tell different stories about their forebears to the same person. But they are all friendly, easy-going, amiable.

Rosie is not in the least ladylike, but very friendly. She smiles all the time and is short and plump, for a Chinese. She wears a *cheong-sam* made of some shiny material, with its skirt slit up the sides to more than half-way up her thighs, and so tight that every movement of her behind is revealed. She could scarcely look more unclothed if she were stark naked. She always goes through the pretence of looking for someone, glancing over the heads of the seated people as if expecting to recognize an acquaintance several tables away. Although she does not look at your table the search for her imaginary acquaintance brings her nearer and nearer. Now she sits in the chair by your side, if there is one, as if by the merest accident, her eyes still questing in the middle distance. She crosses her plump little legs so that, by the merest chance, one thigh is visible almost as far as where it is no longer a thigh at all.

'Hallo, Rosie, Looking for someone?'

'Me? Oh, I thought . . .' She gives a little laugh. 'But never mind. It does not matter.'

'Have a coffee?'

'Yes, thank you.'

For a moment the quest is forgotten. But soon her eyes begin to rove and search once more. She falls silent and seems preoccupied. Presently she rises, perhaps even before she has finished her coffee, and goes once more in search of her imaginary acquaintance. The search is taking her,

I notice, in the direction of two merchant sailors, but they are too drunk to observe her as yet. It will probably be all right when they do, though.

Julia is a Malay. She is a large, fine-looking, handsome girl dressed in the Malay style with flared blouse and tight bright-coloured hobble skirt. Her good looks are rather spoilt by two gold teeth in front and too much make-up carelessly splashed on. She is covered with glittering things, ear-rings, bracelets, necklaces and rings, that flash and wink as she moves. She has a superb carriage and might be a queen the way she sails majestically up and down the rows of tables. She speaks English well but, having learnt most of it from Her Majesty's Forces, she loads it with unfortunate expletives of which she does not know the true meaning. But she does not drift away when she finds you do not mean business and she sits relaxed at your table for a while. You may buy her half a fried chicken if you wish, on which she will fall to with gusto and not speak until she has picked every bone clean and licked her fingers with loud smacking noises. Then she thanks you with a flash of her gold teeth, wiping her fingers on a paper napkin.

'*Terima banyak kaseh.* That was bloody good. Bye-bye.'

She rises and goes her royal way, her splendid breasts sparkling with glass beads. You think of a great ship in full sail.

Two little Malay boys walk down the rows of tables hand in hand. They keep stopping to giggle and ogle and pretend to take great interest in a punch-ball in one of the open shop fronts. This is a great favourite with young servicemen who crowd round it, wearing horrible shirts, showing off their strength. You punch the ball and a hand registers on a dial. If you punch hard enough a bell rings and you get your money back. The possibility, even probability, that the thing may be rigged never seems to worry the contestants. The two boys stand and watch for a little while, still holding hands. They wear very brief shorts, hung low on their hips, and their hair is trained into an elaborate series of undulations and turns up in a duck's tail behind. Inside the punch-ball shop there is a juke-box giving out blasts of rock-'n'-roll, and inside the juke-box there is a mirror. The two boys place themselves in front of this and produce combs from the hip pockets of their shorts. For two or three minutes combing operations as careful and elaborate as the sweeps of a cat's tongue occupy all their attention. They comb with devotion and concentration as though nothing mattered so much in the world as the arrangement of those gleaming black tresses. Perhaps nothing does.

One of the soldiers at the punch-ball looks at them with amused contempt. 'Ow, Claude! Ow nice!' he says in a voice of mincing mockery. The boys turn and bow gravely, as though at a great compliment, and continue on their way, not in the least discomposed.

Every evening the city is invaded by a horde of frustrated, lonely and bored young servicemen, like the ones at the punch-ball. They come from barracks, from camps and from ships. They drift aimlessly into cinemas and into bars, hoping to forget and drown in alcohol and noise their loneliness and homesickness, and to build up defences against the strangeness of their environment. Many clubs and institutions exist, of course, established by well-intentioned authority, for the purpose of helping these young men to forget these familiar aches of youth. The authorities aim to keep them off the streets, out of the bars and away from the fatal attractions of the city, and as much as possible out of contact with the local inhabitants. Accordingly an enormous Naafi has arisen opposite Raffles Hotel. It has its own dance-room and swimming-pool and an interior that seems to wear an air of perpetual, slightly strained brightness, like an anxious air hostess. Select entertainments are constantly being arranged here which begin by being very respectable, but somehow seem to come unstuck as the evening goes on. There is a Union Jack Club and several hostels for seamen, while every air-field, barracks and naval camp has its welfare arrangements, its cinemas and its club rooms with bright chintzes, torn magazines and uncomfortable arm-chairs. But none of these things really keeps the boys away from the bars, although, in the R.A.F. especially, there is a growing addiction to expensive photographic apparatus, ice-cream and young ladies. For in bars you can assert your virility in so many ways. You can make the juke-box obey you and everyone present must drown in the noise of your choosing or get out. You can shout and sing or pick a fight. The little bar girls, who are also hostesses, have just the right mixture of aloofness and friendly accessibility to flatter the male ego. Each male ego thinks that, among all the other egos present, he has just what it takes to break down that air of hard-to-get which is so expertly worn. It is all a question of charm and personality, of course. Technique, my boy! Watch me! Until at last the heat and noise turn to a chill between the shoulder-blades and the male ego vomits itself up in the lavatory. But none of this is quite possible among the chintzes and the potted palms, the masters of ceremony and the small gins-and-oranges of the base or barracks club.

But in Bugis Street everything is possible, and after midnight male egos in their hundreds drift there. Perhaps this ego is just the one that Rosie is looking for. You can tell Auntie all about it and try to get a smile out of Lily. Buy a fried chicken for Julia and laugh at her terrible language. 'What for you always laugh when I speak, you silly bugger?' Or you can just sit there, as I used to, and let time slide past like a dark river, flowing out of nowhere into nowhere, bearing to your feet upon its flood driftwood and frail blossoms. They spin at your feet and glide on again. The stars are kind and look down blandly upon our poor humanity.

The Ebb & Flow
of a National River
by Elizabeth Su

In the heart of Singapore city, there flows a river. It is not a very long river, only 3 kilometres; and it has not always been clean. It was polluted with the scum of civilization, plastic bags, human refuse and even dead cats. But it is, as it was, the pride of Singaporeans, the livelihood of bumboat operators, the bane of environmental cleaners, the source of inspiration for artists, the rendezvous for strolling lovers...

When Sir Stamford Raffles and his entourage rowed up the Singapore River in 1819, its entrance was lined with mangrove swamps. The first hint of the river's past was obvious in the human skulls which littered the river banks, 'some of them old, some of them with hair still remaining, some with teeth still sharp and some without teeth.' Apparently, the pirates of the past had had no qualms about using the river as a dumping ground for incriminating evidence and unwanted cargo. Not to be put off, Raffles negotiated an agreement which led to the beginnings of a British settlement on the island. From then on, the river became the focal point of activity with every man arriving or leaving from its banks.

Even in legend, the story of the founding of Singapore is intertwined with the ebb and flow of the river.

Many centuries ago, according to the *Sejarah Melayu* or Malay Annals, Sang Nila Utama, Son of Raja Iskandar, Ruler of Palembang, took the title of Sri Tri Buana. This prince, while he hunted on a coast spied the gleaming shore of Temasek. He was enchanted and set out to explore

72

it. But a great storm arose and threatened to sink his golden ship. Much was thrown overboard to lighten the vessel but it could not be baled dry. In a desperate attempt, Sri Tri Buana flung his own crown into the sea and miraculously, the storm abated. Landing at Kuala Temasek, the estuary of a river, Sri Tri Buana encountered a strange beast with a red body, a black head and a white breast. On being told that the animal was probably a lion, he decided to establish a settlement at the site of this auspicious omen and named it Lion City — Singapura.

It might be mere coincidence but in 1349, a Chinese trader by the name of Wang Ta-yuan related the incident of a Malay chief who, on digging along the shore, came across a bejewelled cap. Perhaps this cap was the very crown that Sri Tri Buana had jettisoned.

Another early chronicler of Singapore was Munshi Abdullah, Raffles's translator. He noted in his memoirs that there were many rocks at the mouth of the river. Among these was one with a pointed end that looked like a snout of a garfish. The Orang Laut (Sea Gypsies) paid homage to this haunted rock under the implicit threat of being slain by the garfish in the river.

Stories about this rock appear in various versions through the early history of Singapore. According to one ancient chronicle, a Javanese warrior-king, Kritanagara, invaded the island in 1257 A.D. and ordered a monument boasting of his conquest erected at the mouth of the river. There certainly was, in 1819, such a monolith inscribed with unknown characters at the river mouth. Badly worn by tides, it defied all attempts to decipher its message. However, the Bengali sailors who found it while clearing the river mouth were so frightened by the inscription that they would not finish their work. This rock was eventually blown up in 1843 by a government engineer to make way for new construction. Some fragments were then presented to Bengal where it was conjectured that the inscriptions were a record of some Javanese triumph before the conversion of

Malays to Islam.

The authorities, far from displaying proper respect for an artefact of history, sat on the subject in question — literally. In 1848, it was told that the only remaining portion of the stone left in Singapore had been found lying on the verandah of the Treasury, where it was used as a seat by the Sepoy guards and other persons waiting to transact business in the building. It came as no surprise therefore that, due to diligent use and friction, the inscription was nearly erased.

Today, remnants of this ancient monument can be seen in the Singapore and Calcutta Museums.

Another account from 1884 tells of how this rock or one like it was decorated with flags and surrounded by offerings. When the sea wall was built around Fort Fullerton at the mouth of the river, it was destroyed, and the river apparently immediately silted up.

The Singapore River was originally the home of numerous Orang Laut tribes. They lived on their *sampan panjangs*, stream-lined, shallow draught vessels propelled by paddles or lateen mat sails. By the mid-1800s, however, the Orang Laut had disappeared as a distinct community.

Soon after the British made their appearance, the Orang Kallang disappeared to the Pulai River in Johore where most of them died in a smallpox epidemic. The Orang Seletar continued their wandering existence undisturbed until the 1850s when the Johore Straits was subject to more frequent traffic. Some then drifted to peaceful creeks on the Malayan peninsula while the remaining were absorbed into the shore population. Although the Orang Gelams also settled on islands in Keppel Harbour and other Malay villages ashore, a large fleet of Orang Gelam boats remained in the Singapore River, attracting a shifting population of Orang Laut from the Riau-Lingga archipelago. In the late 1840s, the government dispersed this floating village because it obstructed port traffic and was rumoured to have harboured pirates.

The *sampan panjang* soon gave way to double-ended lighters of

Indian design known as *dhonis*. Built and manned by lightermen from South India, they carried cargo from the trading vessels anchored off shore to the quays along the river's length. Their domination was short-lived. By 1867, the Chinese *twakow* (bumboat) had made its appearance and began its monopoly as the river craft for the next 85 years.

There is a story that says the Chinese lighter is modelled after the slipper of Shih Huang Ti, the Chinese Emperor who built the Great Wall.

Once upon a time, there was a Chinese Emperor who worried a lot. He worried about ruling his people. He worried about keeping his country free from strangers. And he worried about his shipbuilders. Now, you might wonder why an Emperor should worry about shipbuilders. It was because Chinese shipbuilders were an industrious lot who liked to go on adventures and see new places and the Emperor certainly did not like that.

One day, the shipbuilders presented their Emperor a plan for a new ship. They said it could sail to the end of the sea to expand the empire. But the Emperor only worried more than ever. He was afraid that if these ships could go far away, they might also return with influences which might bring war to his peace-loving people.

So, instead of approving the plans for the new ship, the Emperor threw his shoe at the shipbuilders and decreed that from hence forth all ships were to be modelled after his royal slipper, a good broad-toed, broad-heeled, broad-soled one.

Lowering his voice and winking to his Prime Minister, the Emperor is supposed to have muttered, "...and it's devilish funny cruising at sea they will be if they adhere to that model." More probably though, he must have shouted, giving vent to his royal rage, "Ship, my foot! Here take this!"

Since that day, so the story goes, Chinese shipbuilders have faithfully followed the imperial fancy and made slipper-shaped boats.

Now we can understand why historians have been referred to the early small boats of Singapore's antiquity as 'shoe boats'.

Whether shoe boats or bumboats, the movement of all boats up and down river was controlled by the tide. The Singapore River is a tidal river and its low bridges designed to facilitate road traffic crossing it also prevented boats from passing under them during high tide.

The mention of this problem cannot pass without remembering one man known in the history of Singapore simply as Captain Faber.

Captain Faber was a government engineer and bridge builder but he is remembered not so much for the structures he built but for a rather preposterous statement he once made. When confronted with the fact that the bridges he had built became barriers for boats at high tide, Captain Faber coolly recommended dredging the river bed to lower the water level!

It was certainly no smooth sailing for him. In 1846, the roof of the covered landing place along the Singapore River which was being erected under his supervision gave way and seriously injured several workmen. The pillars had been too thin and the roof naturally collapsed. It was news and the local newspaper reported on the incident by drawing attention to the engineer-in-charge, and tabulating his various 'accomplishments'.

"First, Faber's Bridge could not maintain its proper position until after several attempts; next the walls of the new market, after it was finished, were found to be cracking most alarmingly in several places, owing to the ends of the building proving too heavy in comparison to the sides, and, from the trecherous nature of the soil, which had not been sufficiently guarded against, beginning to sink very fast. The pediments, which were of an ornamental character, were therefore obliged to be removed, and the building now presents, when viewed from either end, a bald and meagre appearance. The next undertaking of any moment was the new landing place, which has proved equally, or more, unlucky. The new gaol, we hope will afford

Captain Faber an opportunity of redeeming his reputation."

It did not. The gaol eventually had to be rebuilt by convict labour!

Convicts were also used when Captain Collyer began to build Fort Fullerton on the southern side of the river mouth soon after the settlement was founded. But it was not completed till 1858. The fort was armed with 56- and 58-pound guns and included barracks and a house for the officer-in-charge. The road which served it was, not surprisingly, named Battery Road. Captain Collyer, in his zeal, also pulled down the old Government House and levelled the top of the hill to make way for Fort Canning. These two fortresses were practically useless. In fact, the reverberations of practice shots at Fort Fullerton brought down the ceilings of nearby shophouses and godowns.

These unfortunate buildings must have been on Boat Quay which formed an elegant curve once described as being similar to the Regent Street Quadrant. The original buildings have long gone and in their place today stand a row of two- and three-storied shophouses.

There is nothing really outstanding about them. Painted in muted tones, they line the river in humble quietude. One of them is a three-storey shophouse bearing a black wooden sign over its portal. The Chinese characters, boldly carved and goldleafed, reads "Tan Guan Lee".

Owned by the Tan family, the business was established in about 1891. It's founder proprietor was a rice merchant, Lord Tzi Wang; who also established "Wang Lee" along the banks of the Chao Praya in Thailand. Lord Tzi Wang and his brother, Tan Tong Guan, had come to Singapore bearing the official seal of approval from the Chinese Emperor to establish a business.

While Lord Tzi Wang devoted his energies to his business in Thailand, his son and brother cultivated businesses in Singapore and China respectively, cementing the network and importing grain and goods from Burma, Thailand and Indo-China.

"Tan Guan Lee" is only one of many shophouses along the Singapore River. Looking at the stolid but unimpressive facades, one may be tempted to dismiss them disparagingly as common, old shophouses. But they are more than that. A wealth of history resides within their facades and their history is woven inextricably into the tapestry of the wider history of the river.

The River has seen good times and bad times. So has the businesses operating from its banks. Their fortunes have followed the ebb and flow of the tide which exerts its force on the river. They are irrevocably tied up with the destiny of the river and their fate depends on it.

The river was the heart of Raffles's master plan for his settlement. He decreed that the left bank, the adjoining plain and the land on the opposite bank of the river mouth were to be reserved for the cantonment and as an official quarter. The right bank was alloted to the Chinese while the European, Indian and Malay towns were to be situated further inland.

There was the question of where the business quarter should

be. Kampong Gelam, far from the river, was considered but Raffles had his sights set on the swampy north bank, arguing that, if Kampong Gelam were to become the business area, this side of the river would remain unimproved for a hundred years.

So, where there was no natural landing place, Raffles created one. He ordered that a nearby hill be broken up and the earth used to reclaim the swamp. In one tidy operation involving 'two or three hundred labourers' he produced two landmarks: a commercial square (now Raffles Place) on the levelled hill and Boat Quay from the landfill.

River steps were designed to fringe the quay and the sheltered basin immediately became the focal point of trading activity. The merchants built jetties, offices and godown and by 1860, three-quarters of all shipping business transacted through Singapore was done at Boat Quay.

1869. The Suez Canal opened. Coinciding with the shift from sail

79

power to steam driven vessels, this short route to the East represented a revolution in trade. Suddenly the river banks became inadequate and increasing demands led to a new harbour in Tanjong Pagar.

Singapore's trade expanded eightfold between 1873 and 1913 and shifted from the rather exotic wares of the nineteenth century to the bulk movement of primary products, chiefly rubber and tin, but also copra and sugar.

All this was carried in the deep bellies of tongkangs built in shipyards fringing the river. They

would chug to and fro, from ships anchored off-shore to the warehouses along the riverside, to the joy of those who had staked their fortunes on the Singapore River.

In the middle of this ceaseless commercial energy, stands the working man of the river. Coolie, labourer, lighter operator.

Whichever name he goes by, he is the muscle of the river's life, the most vocal, visible and viable *persona* that fueled the trade along quay side and godowns.

But the lighterman's job is an unenviable one of a contract labourer. Their's was an arduous and backbreaking task, hoisting burdens of 200 kilos on their sinewy backs and walking a 20 centimetre wide plank from boat to shore till the holds were empty. All this they endured for $4 per month in the old days. That was deemed adequate in the 1950s when each employee would still be given twenty cents for a hair cut.

They slept on the ground floor of the shophouse or outside along the five-foot-way. In the evenings if there was no work to be done, the lightermen entertained themselves, playing cards and singing, or perhaps listening to heroic tales told by the tentative light of a storyteller's lamp.

The coolies shared a fraternal relationship; one of them would work in the kitchen preparing simple Teochew fare for the worker's daily meal. Breakfast was a communal affair even at 6 a.m. Food was basic: porridge with several savoury dishes, but they ate their fill. They needed their strength for the work ahead.

Two or three doors away was the official opium dispensary where sick coolies produced medical chits and got their dose of opium to alleviate their aches and pains.

Their labour gave the river life. A busy day at Boat Quay would mean fifty-odd bumboats cluttering up the quay, rocking bumper to bumper on the waters. There was always movement. Lorries jockeying for the best position; buyers impatient to inspect goods; foremen shouting instructions; traders haggling and the accountant rapidly clicking his abacus and recording sales. This was the cacophony of trade; the energy of

the river.

Today, the boats are gone. The activity has ceased and the river is silent and still.

In August 1983, a bumboat slipped under Cavenagh Bridge and out to sea. Nothing spectacular about that, since it had passed under it countless times before; except that this time it was for one way only. It represented the hundreds of lighters which had operated along the river for decades to leave its shelter for good. They had all been assigned new wharfs along Pasir Panjar; the river was to be prepared for a new role.

In the heart of Singapore is a river. It is not a very long river. It is not very clean. But it is a national river.

And perhaps because it is so, many parties are taking an interest in it. The Ministry of Environment, the Urban Redevelopment Authority and the Singapore Tourist promotion Board have all made it their concern. One national economic advisor has dismissed the river as a 'sewer' while a citizen hailed it as a 'cultural heritage'. Conservationists have plans to turn the river once again into '*Bu Ye Tian*' — a place of ceaseless activity in the mould of San Francisco's Fisherman's Wharf or Boston's Feneuil Hall. Sportsmen have swum in it, rowed on it and fished its waters. Romantics and journalists have personified the river as either Old Man River or *la grand dame*. Visionaries have plans to make it the most exciting and lively stretch of waterfront in South East Asia.

But for the moment, the river is at rest.

The Singapore River is a river of shifting moods, but certainly a river with a personality of its own. It was destined to be a nation's vitality and rhythm, constant as the tide which washes her banks. It has seen change and change does not perturb it. It was, after-all, once a pirate-harbouring tidal inlet transformed into a powerful corridor of commerce.

There is change ahead and the river knows it.

She is silent and she waits.

In the heart of the nation, the river flows on.

THE PADANG
"THE GREEN GREEN GRASS OF HOME"
by Ilsa Sharp

THINK of the great squares, palaces and plazas, the meeting places of the world — London's Picadilly Circus, Amsterdam's Dam Square, the Champs Elysees in Paris, Time Square in New York, Piazza San Marco in Venice...

Their match in Singapore is the Padang.

Where else in Asia but Singapore could you find a 73-storey skyscraper heralding the twenty-first century jammed next to a 100 year-old hotel, Raffles, an even older Gothic cathedral, St Andrew's, a City Hall and a Sup-

reme Court whose very pomposity of design trumpet the 1930s zenith of the British Empire — and in the midst of all these, the timeless tableau of a cricket match played out on a sward as verdant as any English village green?

Beyond that green — the Padang — lie the restless comings and goings of one of the world's busiest and most romantic harbours.

Substitute sailing junks for the sophisticated container-ships of today, hackney carriages for the motor traffic milling around the

Padang, gaze through the haze of nostalgia, and this would be a timeless moment indeed.

In those far-off days before the dawn of the twentieth century, "The Turn" around the Padang at twilight was a daily social ritual for the colonial settlers.

Bonneted and crinolined mothers chaperoned their pasty young daughters in horse-drawn carriages circling the green. Eyeing the eligible bachelors playing games or exercising their horses all the while, the women would turn aside only to bob in excited snobbery as they caught sight of the Governor and his equipage through the yellow-blossomed angsana trees lining the Esplanade.

Over at Scandal Point, roughly where the Singapore Recreation Club stands now, the older men exchanged gossip, scandalous or otherwise, discussed the market, politics and trade, and generally grumbled into their beards.

The Padang then was a mere 73 metres (80 yards) wide — only in 1890 was it almost doubled by land reclamation. "If the tide was high, you batted; if it was low,

you asked your opponents to start their innings," said the cricketers in those days.

Long before Raffles' arrival, the Padang had been earmarked for sport and recreation. The Malay and Indonesian seafarers who first settled the island would race their sailing ships, nifty little pirate perahus, koleks and sampan panjangs, in annual sea sports on the waters just beyond the Padang. Today's Chinese dragon-boat races along the Singapore River echo this tradition.

The Europeans took the cue to start their own annual New Year Regatta in 1834, expanding it to a full-scale Sports Day by 1839.

All the tomfoolery typical of the English fun-fair, the church bazaar and the public school sports day were on display.

Three-legged races, sack races, egg-and-spoon races, greased-pole climbing, tug-of-war contest, even pig-catching, goose-chasing, eating competitions and ducking for coins in tubs of molasses competed for the attention of startled Asian onlookers with more staid horse-racing, athletics and football.

New Year's Eve had ended with a spectacular waterfront fireworks display; the Day itself culminated in a grand ball at Government House.

Small wonder the local Tamil-Indian name for the Padang meant very simply, "The January Place."

The Padang seems to be eternal. Yet in truth, the only thing constant in Singaporeans' lives since full Independence in 1965 has been change.

Elements of the city's original nineteenth-century urban design have put up an obstinate resistance however, remaining until today, the 1980s.

The Padang, that green lung airing the heart of the city, is one such survivor, a reassuring link in the chain of historical continuity.

Two nineteenth-century sports clubs, the one-time colonial British Singapore Cricket Club at the Padang's western end and the one-time Eurasian Singapore Recreation Club at the eastern end, act as joint guardians of this precious emerald set amid a bristling crown of skyscrapers.

"Padang" is the Malay for "playing field". The Singapore Padang has been that of course, but also far more.

Here is a public space for all occasions, a place where the great dramas of this island-nation's history have been played out.

Riot and revolution, the speeches of the founding fathers, of conquerors and the conquered, rulers and the ruled, the parades of the defeated and despairing as well as the triumphant, even the pop concerts of the new post-Independence generation — the Padang has seen them all.

As Prime Minister Lee Kuan Yew himself told it in a 1970 speech, a United Nations foreign adviser once pointed to the existence of the Padang as a key reason for foreign investors' confidence in the Republic of Singapore. It had survived the struggle for Independence.

The Padang was, this adviser told Singapore's new government in 1960, a symbol of political stability and maturity:

"When people see this, they think, 'This place must be reasonable and sane. It has not been stricken by madness.'"

"Fortunately, next to (the statue

of Raffles) is an open field (the Padang). It has not been tarmaced over. There is no square like other places which tried to imitate the Kremlin Red Square. You still grow grass. It is green and cut. It costs the Government nothing."

"That is very important to people who are thinking of investing their money in Singapore. When they see these things in Singapore, they have that indefinable quality called confidence. You can destroy it overnight but it takes a long time creating it."

In a striving, newly industrialised and until only recently "Third World" nation like Singapore, it is indeed a miracle that such prime city land should be left empty, the sole preserve of sportsmen.

Many have cast lascivious eyes on the Padang's virgin space in the past, but fortunately to no avail.

Singapore's first town-planner, Sir Thomas Stamford Bingley Raffles of the British East India Company, himself reserved the Padang — then known as the Plain, or "Raffles Plain" — for his own government, military and other official buildings when drawing up his 1822 blueprint. It was then no more than a scrubby open space dotted with myrtle and rhododendron.

But the European merchants, backed by Raffles' first Resident of Singapore, Colonel William Farquhar, built their homes around the green and forced its reservation as an open space for public use.

In 1830, the Governor, Robert Fullerton, considered putting the whole area up for sale to developers. But once again, the worthy burghers of Singapore protested, threatening to buy the site over for themselves and hold it vacant.

And in the 1850s, the original design for St Andrew's Cathedral envisaged building it on the Padang. Lobbied by the merchants yet again, Bishop Wilson of Calcutta, then spiritual guardian of Singapore, was prevailed upon to refuse consecration of this site.

In the late 1930s, a projected government re-vamp of the Padang would have converted it into a grandiose "Plaza", moving the Cricket Club to the eastern end and removing the Recreation

Club to another site altogether. Because of World War II, this plot came to naught.

The war saw the Padang littered with broken masonry and burned-out cars, the results of Japanese bombing raids. Fearful of enemy plane or parachute landings, Singapore's defenders seeded the green with ugly steel pylons. Some say the war dead still lie beneath the Padang turf today.

After a brief flirtation with sport on the Padang in 1943, the desperate Japanese, seeing their triumph fade towards 1945, wounded the already neglected cricket pitch with deeply-gashed trenches.

But once again the Padang was to witness history in the making when Admiral Lord Louis Mountbatten, Supreme Allied Commander of Southeast Asia, formally received the Japanese surrender on the steps of City Hall, Septem-

Japanese troops filling trenches on the Padang after Liberation.

ber 12 1945.

Vengeful Singapore Chinese, together with the liberating British, gloated at the sight of their one-time conquerors the Japanese being forced to labour at filling in the very trenches they had dug into the Padang during their Occupation of Singapore.

The turbulent 1950s and '60s saw yet another series of assaults on the integrity of the Padang. The fiery young nationalists fighting for Singapore's independence from the British talked loudly of taking the Padang back "for the people" from the elitist sports clubs leasing and controlling it. But this fire too died down with time.

Since thousands of Singaporeans crammed the Padang in June 1959 to hear their newly elected People's Action Party leaders, still in charge today, there has been natural and painless social evolution. The Padang today really does belong to the people of Singapore.

Asian sportsmen play on it. National, representative sporting bodies have access to it. The annual 9 August National Day parades are held on it. Open-air variety and symphony concert audiences use it. In 1985, the Cricket Club even held a charity funfair extravaganza on it, raising S$85,000 for the Community Chest of Singapore.

And as always in the past, people walk across it, along the path joining St Andrew's Road to Connaught Drive and the Esplanade, a path which demarcates the division between the Padang held by the Recreation Club and that belonging to the Cricket Club.

Time was, even up to the 1960s, when Bugis sailors from the remote Celebes islands of Indonesia would sit on the Padang patching their sails, waiting for the monsoon winds to change and take their trading ships back home.

The crowds for matches on the Padang today are not quite as large or vociferous as they seem to have been before 1959. Cricket is no longer taught at school and betting on soccer is an illicit pleasure.

Almost oblivious of the Cenotaph commemorating victims of the 1914–18 War, the nineteenth-century cherub-entwined Tan

Bugis sailors mending sails on the Padang, circa 1946.

Kim Seng Fountain and the ungainly, funnel-like Lim Bo Seng Memorial to the memory of the torture-murdered anti-Japanese resistance leader by that name, young Singaporeans today wander carefree along the shady garden paths of the Esplanade and Queen Elizabeth Walk on the southern side of the Padang.

Here are lovers cuddling on park benches, their seniors simply *jalan-jalan, makan angin* (strolling around and taking the air), a few fanatic gamblers, idlers and medi-

tators — and dedicated gourmands lured by the pungent odours of the satay or kebab-style charcoal barbecues at the "Satay Club" food centre.

The Padang has become just a familiar backdrop, taken for granted. Yet for most Singaporeans it is unthinkable that it should one day not be there.

The inviting empty space that the Padang is surely must still figure in the dreams of Singaporean developers, however, as it did even in the nineteenth century: just as the Balinese can leave no surface undecorated, so Singaporeans can leave no space undeveloped.

A celebrated April Fool's Joke published by the *Straits Times* in 1982 came close to the bone.

Under the unlikely heading "Hot-air High-rise," the 1 April edition of the paper declared in a lengthy and detailed feature article that there were government plans to "transform the Padang in front of the City Hall and Supreme Court from a sleepy football field into a dazzling new heart for the city."

Even though most Singaporeans were already jaded with announcements of the demolition of this landmark and the development of another, they leaped to the telephone as one man to protest against such sacrilege. Switchboards were jammed with complaints.

That crisis was not for real. But it will take conscious care and alert stewardship to protect the Padang for ever, not to be "stricken by madness" as that United Nations adviser put it in 1960.

Whether the Padang survives in the long-distant future will be the litmus test of the new Singaporean's sensitivity to history, of his feeling for eternity and "that indefinable quality called confidence."

"I keep forgetting – is it up and along or down and across in hara-kiri?"

The Fortress Falls
by Kate Caffrey

AMONG the films in London that week was the zany classic *Hellza-poppin*. This matched Singapore's situation better than another release, *Blood and Sand*: on the Island the sand might give place to mud and swamp, but the blood was there in plenty.

By Wednesday February 11 1942, the two fighting areas had come closer and closer together, moving in upon the village of Bukit Timah. One pair of defending brigades, the 22nd Australian and the 44th Indian, had fallen back between the Kranji and Jurong Rivers, leaving the western part of the Island to the enemy; the 27th Australian Brigade with part of the 11th Indian Division and several regiments from the 18th British, had been pushed back in sections from the Causeway-Kranji area and the west side of the Naval Base towards the precious reservoirs.

One particular hill in the Mandai district seemed bewitched: two sets of troops had left it in a hurry without being attacked and a third had shied at attacking it when it was empty. Within forty-eight hours of the invasion some of the Argyll, and Sutherland Highlanders were cut off two miles in advance of the British lines and began to struggle back piecemeal to their base. One group ordered to hold the pipeline now consisted of a corporal and two privates, ragged, exhausted and burnt by the sun. Advised to get some sleep inside the British lines the corporal replied that if these three were the last of their battalion he was the senior NCO and they had been told to hold the pipeline, whereupon "all three turned back toward the enemy." Gordon Bennett inexplicably moved the 27th Australians during Wednesday morning without telling either Malaya Command or III Corps, which left a single Australian company and a Baluch regimental battalion to hold the Mandai road and four reduced battalions to try to recapture Bukit Timah village, into which the Japanese had now penetrated.

Singapore town was in absolute chaos: long trailing lines of native civilians were clogging the roads, already blocked by traffic, towards the eastern part of the Island. They carried their belongings on their backs, in handcarts or abandoned rickshaws, in one case in an empty coffin. Those who were trying to drive somewhere on official business found that it took over an hour to go two or three miles. All the hospitals had received direct hits, and one of them, a group of huts at Tyersal Park, was burnt to the ground; most of the people there were killed, either in the fire or by machine-gunning from the air. The St. Andrew's Cathedral was filled with stretcher cases.

On Tuesday a rumour started that the nurses were to be evacuated, and the chief of the civilian medical services, Dr R. B. MacGregor, got in touch with the Governor to see if this could possibly be true. Sir Shenton Thomas checked with Percival his Chief of Staff Officer and reported back to MacGregor that no such idea had been considered. A heavy air raid now opened up on the docks and the officer in charge there telephoned Brig. Ivan Simson, the Chief Engineer to ask for advice: he said that the senior European officials of the Harbour Board had left the Island on orders from the Governor. Simson at once checked with Sir Shenton and the Governor admitted that it was true, he had been told by Whitehall to send the Harbour Board officials out as they were experts and needed in India, and by an oversight he had forgotten to tell Simson.

The responsibility for destroying the docks machinery now lay with the ARP under Tim Hudson of Dunlop's, who was asked to start the demolitions that afternoon, but the Japanese beat him to it. They came over in precision formation, dropped their bombs as usual all together, hit a fuel dump, a rubber warehouse, a sugar warehouse, set fire to shops in the Keppel Road and a Chinese junk out in the water, and threatened a sawmill and a timber works. A shell fired at the same time exploded on a paint shop and set it alight. Mr Hudson drove some casualties to the General Hospital where he found a mass burial going on, the many dead being placed in two huge pits.

SINGAPORE SLING

It is difficult to sort out the events of those last days into any kind of orderly narrative, partly because plans were changed or not made clear and partly because few people kept any precise record of their actions. Even if they had, it would give a false impression: the movements were never co-ordinated and never orderly. Told to hold in one place, a commander would do so for a while and then inexplicably pull back. One group of Australians close to the Causeway held on splendidly, their CO having been refused permission to withdraw; in the morning the Japanese gave up trying to push further in at that place. Yamashita waited an hour or two, asked for a fresh reconnaissance report, and found to his amazement that the Australians had gone. The CO had withdrawn them, saying he had permission, Gordon Bennett indignantly denied giving it, and whoever was to blame the result was that a gap lay open where yesterday there had been stubborn and successful resistance. It was a carbon copy of the withdrawal on the previous night from the Jurong Line. In the light of events like these it is not surprising that Archibald Wavell, Supreme Comander of the Australian British and Dutch Allied Command wrote later: "I left Singapore on the morning of 11 February without much confidence in any prolonged resistance."

The official Orders of the Day, including Wavell's own, still called for all out fighting and he referred to the Americans at Bataan, to the Russians and the Chinese. As it turned out Bataan was overrun in the end, and as for Russia and China, neither of them was really comparable to an island not much bigger than the Isle of Wight. Incidentally, a rumour that spread during the campaign claimed that the War Office had actually sent out maps of the Isle of Wight, though it wasn't made clear whether this was supposed to have happened by accident or whether by design on the principle that anything was better than nothing and supplies of the correct maps were short. The frightening thing about this apparently silly story is that considering all the mistakes that had been made, it might just conceivably (people felt) have been true.

On the Wednesday the Japanese Comander, Tomoyuki Yamashita, had a letter for Percival dropped from a plane. It was a courteously worded request that he should recognise the situation as hopeless and give in without further delay. As a matter of fact speed was essential to Yamashita as well. His Chief of Supply had warned him that stocks of ammunition and petrol were running dangerously low and it would be as well to bring matters to a close as soon as he could. He thought carefully and decided to bluff it out. The aircraft went on raiding, the guns went on firing as though both were inexhaustible and supplies would last for ever. Percival telegraphed the gist of Yamashita's message to Wavell, adding that he did not propose to reply as he had no means of dropping a message; the answers "would of course in any case be negative."

There was still a dribble of people leaving the Island. The Governor took over the *Straits Times* as a government publication and 7,000 single quarto sheets appeared in print on Thursday morning, the lead story consisting simply of the official communiqué, stating that "enemy pressure slackened during the night," that "no change in the situation" was reported from various places. They were piously hoping "to stabilise our position." In a way it was no more unreal than the report that day in *The Times* which quoted a man from Nova Scotia saying in Singapore that the Japanese were "scared to death of cold steel." The *Guardian*, under the headline "Singapore's Fate," said that the Japanese claimed to have entered the city area; "this may relate to penetration of the north-western suburbs."

Captain Russell-Roberts, hearing that all troops were to come back inside the defensive perimeter as they were holding their own nowhere except for the 1st Malay Regiment stubbornly clinging on near Pasir Panjang, went into the town to say goodbye to his wife who was leaving at three that afternoon on a small ship called the *Mata Hari*, and then "drove like mad" to the Golf Course where the rest of his regiment was to be found. They were about to be sent forward of the Kay Siang Road to "fight it out to the end." It took longer to move than they had expected and they did not reach the new position until after first light on Friday. During Thursday, Government House had its worst shelling so far, killing twelve of the domestic staff.

Heavy fighting went on that day around the village of Nee Soon, the Imperial Guards hammering away at a regiment from Baluchistan that gave a good account of itself in spite of being faced by tanks, which were now coming over the Causeway which the Japanese had not taken long to repair. The perimeter line was large when it came to numbers of troops defending it, but small to contain the administrative units which now had no work to do but were not given other jobs and were still cluttered up by enormous quantities of useless equipment. In all the muddle there was no way of keeping security, and Japanese agents went on sending their reports out by radio with complete confidence. Friday the thirteenth dawned fine and clear. In his ARP post at Tiong Bahru school, where he had slept in the headmaster's study, Tim Hudson was just contemplating breakfast of corned beef, bread, and stewed tea, and reading the second edition of the Governor's paper with the words printed across the top: "Singapore must stand; it *shall* stand" when bomber planes droned overhead and a stick of bombs fell across the school. When Mr Hudson picked himself up from the floor and staggered dazedly outside he found the building half demolished, three cars wrecked, and seven people dead, among them his own houseboy. The ARP post was shifted into the College of Medicine where the wardens were told to bury the dead "anywhere, anyhow" — "It was like the Black Death all over again." Since the telephone kept cutting out, Chinese dispatch riders carried the messages, most incoming ones reading: "Japanese approaching, please give instructions."

On that Friday, accompanied by a mass of hasty consultations, list-compiling and altering, argument, persuasion, recrimination and refusal, about three thousand supposedly key people were shipped out in a flotilla of small craft to destinations in Java and Sumatra where their skills might be useful. Among them went several who had been ordered to stay at their posts till the last, including Group Captain Nunn, head of the Public Works Department. Others who went included Rear Admiral Spooner and Air Vice-Marshall Pulford.

Much comment, verbal and written, since then has attempted to work out the rights and wrongs of these individual departures, but the whole question is academic: the ships never reached freedom. Some were sunk as they left the Island, some were captured at sea, some surrendered, some lost their way in the dark and made landfall or small islands where the people on board managed to get ashore but eventually died of illness or starvation or were picked up by the Japanese and brought back.

Pulford and Spooner died, so did Nunn, though he got a lot further than most — he and his wife, arrived in Sumatra, went aboard an old Dutch steamship, sailed for Colombo and were lost when the ship went down in four minutes after a torpedo hit from a Japanese submarine. Mrs Nunn was put in the single lifeboat with eighty others but only four survival long enough to be captured and only one of those, Lieutenant Gibson, lived to tell the tale after the war. Captain Russell-Roberts' wife was captured (his baby daughter had been safely taken to England by friends), and died in captivity.

On Friday evening the Governor left Government House for the more secure shelter of the Singapore Club. Lady Thomas, who had been very ill for some days with amoebic dysentery, was taken out first by ambulance. The stately white house, now under shelling so constant that no one dared to go upstairs, was almost empty, a ghost of the splendid past already. Sir Shenton made a quick trip upstairs to grab a few clothes which he stuffed into a suitcase while his ADC in the kitchen "shovelled any tinned food he could find into a hold all." The two men eventually drove off down the long drive, where the sentry at the gates presented arms as the Governor passed through for the last time.

The Singapore Club was crowded, four or five sleeping in single rooms, queueing for meals (dinner that Friday was corned beef with potato salad out of a tin, and tea made with tinned milk), while the whole of the ground floor was full of wounded for whom the impossibly overworked nurses fetched water from a standpipe out in the street. Over at the Dunlop warehouse Mr Hudson (his dinner that night was sardines and baked beans, with "a stiff brandy") had just arrived to make his nightly check for the European manager when he was visited by four Chinese who offered him half a million dollars in cash for the thousand tons of rubber the warehouse contained. The Chinese told him they had a cargo boat ready to take the rubber to Java, if they didn't take it away the Japanese would get it and they knew how much there was. The rubber belonged to all sorts of people who could not be traced as it had been built up for weeks from shipments sent out of Malaya but, of course, it was not Mr Hudson's property and he simply couldn't do it. The four Chinese, in their tidy white suits, shrugged regretfully, picked up all the bundles of notes and put them back into their briefcases and Mr Hudson saw them out.

Captain David James had had a fairly eventful day. He was in Orchard Road when a stick of bombs exploded across it, setting fire to a petrol station which blazed up in seconds and punting two cars into the air like footballs. They bounced several times and burst into flames. One house collapsed under a direct hit and "looked like a caved-in slaughterhouse." No local ARP people seemed to be around so Captain James rushed off to find an ambulance. He found dozens of them parked by the Cathedral and sent some off to Orchard Road. Moving about in the streets was harder than ever as the town was clogged with people.

In the Municipal Building there were "solid blocks of Australians sitting on the stairs."

On paper, Captain James supposed, Singapore could have held out for many days; but not like this, in the actual conditions of muddle and damage, looting and despair, with the bombs and shells crashing down all the time and the thick black smoke pouring up. Great holes had been smashed in the roads and buildings and telegraph poles stuck grotesquely out of the wreckage, cars and lorries choked every street and sporadic bursts of firing were heard inside the city itself, some of these coming from troops firing at suspected infiltrators. At the Woodleigh pumping station the engineer and his wife were still working hard to keep the water supply going, but more and more it was running to waste out of holes in the pipes.

The hard-pressed fighting troops were being split into smaller and smaller pockets of resistance, the Bedfordshires losing six officers and twenty-six men of one regiment in the first five days. Grimly counting their shrinking numbers, they felt that they "never had a chance to fight." Captain (now Lieutenant-Colonel) Reginald Burton of the 4th Norfolks knew that his men felt they had "done as well as could be expected" in their fighting, especially against an opponent who had the "advantage of position" and good air cover. Knowing that instead of pushing the Japanese off the Island they had been made to withdraw puzzled and depressed them. They had been in quite a good defensive place, and were pulled back only a short distance, where they had to "dig in and wire all over again"; this was "rather last straw." If they could have stayed where they were and allowed the enemy to walk into their fire it would have been better, he thought.

At this stage Captain Burton found himself envying the men who had been wounded and sent to hospital — they were honourably out of the situation, though "that they were in reality far from being out of it didn't enter my head." If any of them were in the Alexandra Military Hospital they were in a far worse state than Captain Burton. The Malay Brigade had held on valiantly for two days at Pasir Panjang, the ridge protecting the Alexandra area, and were now almost wiped out. The Japanese overwhelmed the remnants of them, making straight for the hospital, where a young lieutenant named Weston met them on the steps, carrying a white flag. He was killed at once and the Japanese went through the hospital and killed most of the patients and staff inside, including one man on the operating table. About two hundred of the patients were herded into the old servants' quarters and left there for the night. All but three were killed when a shell scored a direct hit on the building.

During the day, Captain James picked up two very precise Japanese maps and passed them on to HQ. On the flagged veranda of the guardhouse at Fort Canning he handed them in, but the reaction was one of "no interest."

Fort Canning had been having a bad day too, Percival called a meeting at two in the afternoon for all the divisional commanders and staff officers to discuss counter-attack possibilities, which all the commanders opposed. They had to consider their exhausted, hard-pressed troops as well as the civilian population, faced now with the prospect of street fighting. Percival was certain that the end was near, but thought they could manage to hang on for a little longer. He telegraphed Wavell that the Japanese were now "within five thousand yards of the seafront" — the whole town area was now within range of their field artillery. There was danger of running out of water and losing food stocks if the enemy overran them. He quoted the commanders' opinion about the state of the troops.

We would all earnestly welcome the chance of initiating an offensive, even though this would only amount to a gesture, but even this is not possible, as there are no troops who could carry out this attack. In these conditions it is unlikely that resistance can last more than a day or two. My subordinate commanders are unanimously of the opinion that the gain of time will not compensate for extensive damage and heavy casualties which will occur in Singapore town. As Empire overseas is interested I feel bound to represent their views. There must come a stage when in the interests of the troops and civil population further bloodshed will serve no useful purpose.

This telegram bristles with unanswered, and unanswerable, questions. Was it really true that *all* the troops were too exhausted? Why say "earnestly" when one looks for the word "cagerly"? Why was it so clear that "this would only amount to a gesture"? "No troops who could carry out this attack"? Just how unanimous were all the subordinate commanders? What views of the Empire overseas are represented in this message? And (the sixty-four-dollar question) how many lives were saved and whose, by caving in then, now that it is known what happened afterwards? What made Percival think that bloodshed would cease when the fighting stopped?

Wavell's reply was uncompromising.

You must all fight it out to the end as you are doing. But when everything humanly possible has been done some bold and determined personnel may be able to escape by small craft ....

One bold and determined person at least was preparing to do this. Gordon Bennett (who had privately cabled the Australian Prime Minister that if the Japanese got into the town he was going to surrender "to avoid further needless loss of life" without saying a word about this to anyone in Malaya Command), had for some time been working out plans for his own escape. He had discussed the subject with the Sultan of Johore, with whom he had become friendly; the Sultan had entertained Gordon Bennett to meals in his palace and had given the General many presents (on January 28 an entry in Gordon Bennett's diary read: "He entertained me at lunch and appreciated the visit. As usual he displayed his generosity by presenting me with gifts"). Gordon Bennett had asked the Sultan to let him have a boat to escape by if the need arose. In his opinion it had arisen now.

Wavell cabled a summary of Percival's situation to Churchill. It went against every grain of Churchill's nature to say so, but he had no choice any more, and had reluctantly to signal back that in agreement with General Brooke, Chief of the Imperial General Staff, he realised:

You are of course sole judge of the moment when no further result can be gained at Singapore, and should instruct Percival accordingly.

Wavell meanwhile had signalled Percival that the fight must go on.

SINGAPORE SLING

You must continue to inflict maximum damage on enemy for as long as possible by house-to-house fighting if necessary. Your action in tying down enemy and inflicting casualties may have vital influence in other theatres. Fully appreciate your situation, but continued action essential.

Sir Shenton Thomas weighed in at the same time with a message to the Colonial Office.

General Officer Commanding informs me that Singapore City now closely invested. There are now one million people within radius of three miles. Water-supplies very badly damaged and unlikely to last more than twenty-four hours. Many dead lying in the streets and burial impossible. We are faced with total deprivation of water, which must result in pestilence. I have felt that it is my duty to bring this to notice of General Officer Commanding.

The lowered morale was not apparent among the men of Captain Russell-Robert's party who had spent Friday less than a mile to the rear of the Alexandra Hospital, digging in high spirits, surrounded by plenty of supplies in a private house they had taken over as HQ, which was well fitted with a complete set of modern furniture and had a small car in the garage. The men set up guns on the verandas and anti-craft spotters in the bathrooms and sent out foraging patrols.

Buller Camp near by was on fire and so were the oil installations not far off. Over by the reservoirs the 11th Indian Division, or what was left of it, was "still standing firm"; on its left the 5th Norfolks and the 2nd Cambridgeshires, "heavily engaged" throughout the weekend "until the moment of capitulation," "did not flinch." To all the defending troops who were not in the upper echelons of command, that is to say to every soldier from the colonel to the private, the idea of surrender had never occurred. They were all caught absolutely unawares and to the many who wept when the news eventually reached them it was a heartbreaking experience.

Yamashita had his thoughts, too, which he wrote in his diary.

My attack on Singapore was a bluff — a bluff that worked. I had 30,000 men and was outnumbered more than three to one. I knew that if I had to fight long for Singapore, I would be beaten. That is why the surrender had to be at once. I was very frightened all the time that the British would discover our numerical weakness and lack of supplies and force me into disastrous street fighting.

Percival, no bluffer, never imagined that Yamashita could have been worried, and estimated the Japanese forces at about 100,000, indignantly refusing to believe that he could have been forced back to the wall by a smaller army than his own. He seems to have thought at one time that the Japanese were fewer in number, for his Order of the Day of February 10 said: "It will be a lasting disgrace if we are defeated by an army of clever gangsters, many times inferior in numbers to our own"; but by the end of that last week he had come round to the belief that all this brilliant and confident advance, carried out so quickly, could only have been accomplished by an enormous body of troops. He could not know how Yamashita's men were short of water, down to a hundred rounds of shells for each field gun and less for the heavy guns, and were approaching, just as Percival's soldiers were, the limit of endurance at which Wavell thought surrender could no longer be put off.

Short or not, Yamashita was still keeping up the pressure. It seemed by now that the air raids went on all day so that Buckeridge and his squads from the Fire Department never had a break. Some fires blazed while others smouldered sullenly on. There were constant outbreaks too among the warehouses where rubber, sugar and paint were stored. Perhaps the most dramatic incident occurred when a warehouse full of Chinese New Year firecrackers caught alight and the fireworks banged off in all directions. The car park on Collyer Quay caught a cloud of incendiary bombs that burned out hundreds of vehicles. The oddest fire was the one on the Pulo Saigon Bridge over the Singapore River, described by Mr Buckeridge as "a bloody great fire where no fire could possibly be"; a burning oil slick floated up the river on the tide, setting fire to the packed sampans and then to the oil dripping down the bridge from broken oil-pipes that ran along it. "Constructed entirely of steel girders," wrote Noel Barber, "this ancient Meccano-like structure ... was ablaze from end to end." Crowds inured by now to fires stood staring in astonishment as the lace-like ironwork and the asphalt roadway through it slowly burned itself out by ten o'clock that night.

The looters were having a field day. Even the Bishop of Singapore repaired a punctured wheel on his car by pinching a tyre off an abandoned vehicle. Jack Bennitt bought razor blades in every shop that sold them. Groups of men stripped deserted market stalls bare. Through all this, rickshaw men hopefully offered "sightseeing tours." There was a rush on Kelly and Walsh's bookshop, and another rush to get (of all places) to the dentist. Scuffles broke out in tobacco shops where Europeans who had stopped bothering about stocks of food were trying to pile up stocks of cigarettes. The manager of Robinson's issued two free sets of clothes to every European child.

On Saturday night, before going to bed, the Governor wrote in his diary: "Much quieter night in the Club."

Captain James kept on wondering why the 18th British Division had been sent to Singapore. It had only completed its disembarkation on January 29, just over a fortnight ago, and in any case it had never been used as a division. Arriving in pieces it was thrown into the battle in pieces "until it lost its value as a fighting force under its commander, Major-General Beckwith-Smith." The Captain wrote later – much later – that "one-third of this gallant Division died, not in the fighting but as prisoners of war."

In the different patches of action the dawn conferences of Sunday February 15 all took the same line of dogged persistence. Colonel Jimmy Larkin told his men: "Gentlemen, we fight, and if necessary die, in our present position." Brigadier Stewart of the Argylis spoke to his small group, two officers and fifty men "black and greasy from fire-fighting," and reminded them of his two promises, never to order them into battle without enough guns and never to say Go On, only Come On. He had to break the first promise now, there were only too clearly not enough guns, but the second promise still held. Would they, he asked, come into this last battle with him? Nobody spoke. Slowly the men all rose to their feet and stood waiting. The Brigadier led them of towards the guns in the distance.

Colonel Larkin's men were under fire by this time. Shells burst in the garden of the HQ, sending shovefuls of black earth flying in at the windows. The riflemen, heartened by having some real work to do at last, fired away enthusiastically.

But it was all useless. Wavell's last cable had come in at Fort Canning.

So long as you are in position to inflict losses and damage to enemy and your troops are physically capable of doing so you must fight on. Time gained and damage to enemy are of vital importance at this crisis. When you are fully satisfied that this is no longer possible I give you discreation to cease resistance .... Whatever happens I thank you and all troops for your gallant efforts of last few days.

It was the twelfth birthday of Percival's daughter Dorinda, and he started the day by going to Holy Communion, celebrated in the Fort. He was not the only one. Places of worship were crammed that morning, and dozens of services were held in hospitals. At nine-thirty Percival held a short meeting, lasting only twenty minutes, in one of the Fort's bomb-proof rooms, with the senior commanding officers, and he listened quietly as each one gave his appreciation of how matters stood. They were very well turned out in their fresh uniforms — it is curious how centuries-old habits persist — and their verdicts were unanimously negative. Gordon Bennett recorded in his diary: "Silently and sadly we decided to surrender."

The melancholy formalities of capitulation were straightforward enough. Yamashita had made them known in the letter dropped for Percival on Wednesday, Japanese Empire Day. It requested the "parliamentaire" to be sent to the Bukit Timah Road carrying a large white flag and the Union Jack. The two men selected to carry out this distasteful task were the Colonial Secretary Hugh Fraser and the Chief

SINGAPORE SLING

Adminstrative Officer Brigadier Newbiggin.

Knowing what Yamashita's own position was like at the time it is interesting to see how he expressed himself in the letter to Percival.

Your Excellency:

I, the High Command of the Nippon Army based on the spirit of Japanese chivalry, have the honour of presenting this note to Your Excellency advising you to surrender the whole force in Malaya.

My sincere respect is due to your army which, true to the traditional spirit of Great Britain, is bravely defending Singapore which now stands isolated and unaided. Many fierce and gallant fights have been fought by your gallant men and officers, to the honour of British warriorship. But the developments of the general war situation has already sealed the fate of Singapore, and the continuation of futile resistance would only serve to inflict direct harm and injuries to thousands of noncombatants living in the city, throwing them into further miseries and honour of war, but also would not add anything to the honour of your army.

I expect that Your Excellency accepting my advice will give up this meaningless and desperate resistance and promptly order the entire front to cease hostilities and will despatch at the same time your parliamentaire according to the procedure shown at the end of this note. If on the contrary, Your Excellency should neglect my advice and the present resistance continued, I shall be obliged, though reluctant from humanitarian considerations, to order my army to make annihilating attacks on Singapore.

On closing this note of advice, I pay again my sincere respects to Your Excellency.

TOMOYUKI YAMASHITA

This may have been a bluff (as it was) but it has the authentic courtly ring ("What is thy name? I know thy quality"). Very different from Major Toyama, who told Captain James after the surrender: "You defied Dai Nippon, you surrendered and must accept the consequences, you should have died fighting like Japanese soldiers; stop complaining and reconcile yourselves to lifelong imprisonment." Of course the Major did not know just how short a line his own army was working on. Yamashita, who had also started that day in prayer (it was Chinese New Years Day, incidentally, and there should have been fireworks), went up to Bukit Timah during the morning to the Chrysanthemum Division HQ. Here Lieutenant-General Renya Mutaguchi reported that the enemy were firing less than before. Yamashita told him to stand by and went back to his own HQ, and some little time later one of Mutaguchi's patrols reported a white flag "among the trees ahead."

If this was Fraser and Newbiggin, it must have been more than a little while later. Carrying Percival's letter to Yamashita and the two flags requested, they set off from Fort Canning at half past seven. Their car had to turn back twice because of craters in the road, and they were held at gunpoint by a British patrol at the Duncan Road. Because of minefields on the Adam Road they had to go forward on foot. It was nearly half past one before they met any Japanese. An armed patrol came out of the rubber by the canal, where orchids flowered on the bank. After a cautious approach and some explanation by the interpreter, the Japanese took quite a time before escorting the British anywhere; they wanted to take photographs. They posed Fraser and Newbiggin and the interpreter to face the light — it was steaming hot and everybody was sweating — and took pictures. When at last they were satisfied and sent for their senior officers who of course came hurrying along from HQ at top speed, it was past two o'clock.

Yamashita would have none of it. He would deal with Percival in person and the firing would not stop until the General came to meet him. He sent a note back with the two British envoys, who were escorted to Adam Road by Japanese troops. Although they were returning over the same ground they had covered coming up, Fraser and Newbiggin were blindfolded, a puzzling precaution and a frightening one, too, as they walked back during a British shell barrage. At the Adam Road barrier the Japanese left them and they got back into the car. At the Stevens Road a British sergeant fired his pistol at them, missing them by a miracle. They re-entered the Fort at just on four in the afternoon.

SINGAPORE SLING

The place chosen by Yamashita for the surrender ceremony was the Ford Works Buiding near Bukit Timah. It was the biggest covered building left sufficiently intact, though it had been damaged by shells and was pocked with bullet-marks, part of the roof had fallen in and many of the windows gaped open, the glass shattered by shot. In that sultry late afternoon the acid smells of burned rubber and petrol and charred wood seeped out across the principal section, now cleared for this meeting. A long table with a white cloth on it stood in the middle, and chalk marks all over the concrete floor showed where all the officers and reporters summoned to witness the ceremony were to stand.

Right up to the last minute Yamashita was nagged by doubts. Was this a trick? Acutely aware of his own position, his men living on two bowls of rice a day, five gallons out of six of everybody's water supply pouring away through holes in the pipes, rifle ammunition down to one hundred rounds a day for every soldier, he worried until the moment of truth, shortly after five-fifteen, when he came into the building and was face to face with his adversary at last. One glance at Percival's tragic expresssion was enough to reassure Yamashita, but he had to make certain; the colossal gamble had paid off, the enemy had let him get away with it, but it had been done by a perilously narrow margin. Time was as precious to him as ever it could have been to Percival, and he simply had to come to terms that day. His men could not have stood up to a really determined counter-attack at that point, and he knew it. Accordingly he came prepared to put the boldest front on it, to drive the hardest of bargains, assumed a fierce, uncompromising attitude, and clipped out his words to the interpreter, Mr Hishikari: "The Japanese Army will consider nothing but unconditional surrender at ten p.m. Nippon time."

This meant half past eight, barely two hours away. Percival said: "I can't guarantee it — we can't submit our final reply before midnight."

Yamashita banged the table with his fist. "Are our terms acceptable or not? We are ready to resume firing."

According to one account, one of Yamashita's aides now put a paper with questions written on it in English in front of Percival. The first question read: "Does the British Army surrender unconditionally?" Another account reported Yamashita as saying: "Answer me briefly — do you wish to surrender unconditionally?" Both accounts record Percival's request to wait until next morning. Yamashita said: "In that case we shall go on fighting until then," and, pointing at Percival, he told Mr Hishikari: "Tell him to answer yes or no."

Percival, weary, anxious and beaten, hesitated; at some point Yamashita asked: "Have you any Japanese prisoners of war?"

"None at all."

"Have you any Japanese civilians?"

"No, they have all been sent to India." (This exchange comes in the Japanese account and seems a little peculiar: if this was so, what about all the informers, infiltrators, fifth columnists? But perhaps it was thought best for the Japanese not to hear about those.)

The big question came again. "Do you consent immediately to unconditional surrender or do you not?"

Percival, with his head bowed and speaking "in a faint voice," said: "Yes".

The instrument of surrender was laid before him. Before signing, Percival asked that the Japanese troops should not enter the city before morning, and agreed that his own troops should be disarmed at once "except for a thousand who would maintain order during the night." Yamashita warned him that any breach of this agreement would start the fighting up again. Then there was a further question. One account gives it as: "Will the Imperial Army protect the women and children and the British civilians?" The other quotes it as: "What about the lives of the civilians, and the British, Indian and Australian troops? Will you guarantee them?" There is a significant difference in the two questions. There is not much variation in the reply.

"Yes. You may be easy about that. I can guarantee them absolutely"; or: "Please rest assured, I shall positively guarantee it."

Percival signed. One account says it was seven o'clock the other that it was ten past six. The two commanders shook hands while the flashbulbs popped and the reporters scribbled in their notebooks. Yamashita wanted to say something kind to his enemy who looked so tired and thin and defeated. He could not speak English, he knew how hard it is to convey any feelings correctly through an interpreter, so he tried to make his meaning clear with a look and a sympathetic handshake.

It is doubtful whether Percival noticed. He stood up very straight as he turned on his heel and left the room. Yamashita picked up his papers.

"It was for Egypt and for Russia," said the *Guardian*, "that we sacrificed Malaya."

Jubilant broadcasts in Berlin and Tokyo reported that Sir Shenton Thomas and his officials had left by air, that most of the British and Australian troops left the Island on Friday for Sumatra, that those remaining, numbers varying between 65,000, 45,000, and 30,000, had quickly been assembled "in the Changi fort." On the Allied side the reaction was stunned disbelief. Franklin Roosevelt sent Churchill what comfort he could. "It gives the well-known back-seat driver a field day, but ... I hope you will be of good heart in these trying weeks."

Samson, seeing that his part would be over by about six, had got all his arrangements lined up to leave the Island, but Percival had forbidden him to go. Gordon Bennett, who consulted nobody, issued an order to his Australians to remain at their posts until eight-thirty the next morning and that foolish actions should not imperil the cease-fire, arranged for new clothing and two days' rations for everybody, and went down to the docks with two officers who were coming with him. He apparently hoped to get to Malacca, but he met a party led by Mr M.C. Hay, Inspector of Mines, and they all got on board a junk which, after a brisk hectoring of the Chinese skipper by Mr Hay, sailed south a few minutes later, leaving behind the dying Lion Gate and the equally dying military career of the Australian commander.

Promptly at eight-thirty the guns fell silent. News of the surrender began to spread, received for the most part with horrified incredulity. Some sought the comfort of food, opening hoarded tins for a "surrender dinner" — one such meal consisted of steak and kidney pie, Christmas pudding and strawberries and cream. Other crowded the space left in the Cathedral among the ranks of wounded and joined in a service led by the Bishop, including, oddly, the hymn "Praise, my soul, the King of Heaven." Mr Hudson packed a bag, picked up a couple of bottles of whisky from the Dunlop warehouse where he had hidden them, and went with Mr Buckeridge of the Fire Service to Robinson's, where there was quite a party. People ate tinned meat and pineapple from the shop kitchens, drank out of restaurant glasses, had baths using the ladies' hairdressing soap and the household department baths, and went to sleep on the luxurious beds and sofas of the furniture department. Among the sleepers there that night was Captain Russell-Roberts.

When last heard of, the Captain was out near Tanglin, where in a last gallant barrage of rifle fire, his men were giving all they had got "for the first and last time" even though the range was too impossibly great. They heard that the white flag had gone forward; darkness fell, quiet and full of rumours. Eventually the surrender message was read out and was received with emotion. The men went in to Singapore by way of River Valley Road, and were quartered in a large building close by Change Alley while the officers went into Robinson's to have their last good sleep for nearly thirteen hundred nights "on those heavenly sofas."

Captain Reginald Burton, who had been slightly hurt in the last bursts of fighting, was lying on a mattress on the floor when the news of the surrender reached him. When he heard that a car with a white flag had been seen heading towards the enemy lines he thought it was "just another story." But finally one of his men came up to him and told him that it was all over. Feeling sick, Captain Burton turned his head away and "lay for a long time, trying to think clearly." The strongest feeling he had was what a waste it had all been — the long voyage, the short battle, and now the prospect of captivity: for how long? involving what?

SINGAPORE SLING

This is not the reaction of a beaten man. Neither was that of Mr Buckeridge, who wrote in his diary:

We'd given up. Or someone had. The gang of men round the table was as weary as I was, but I'm sure that every single one was willing and eager to carry on the struggle. But there was no struggle. It was over. We talked as though we shared a dreadful secret. Dreadful it was, but secret, no. We didn't know what the hell had gone wrong. We were damn sure it wasn't us.

Yamashita gave a cocktail party at HQ, with chestnuts and dried cuttlefish and wine. Later he would accept General Wainwright's surrender of the Philippines. But even in the chaos of war a pattern emerged, for in Tokyo Bay on September 2, 1945, when the Japanese formally surrendered General MacArthur would have both Warnwright and Percival beside him. He would sign his name in fragments, using six pens: one for his wife, one for his aide, one for West Point and one for the Archives, but "the first pen went to Wainwright. Percival got the next one." It made a sort of rounding-off, after the "1,297 days" that lay between now and then.

But that Sunday, Yamashita, emerging from the Ford Works Building, was the man who had found the pot of gold at the end of the rainbow. It had been a staggering feat of arms on his part. Against all the odds, all the expectations, operating on a shoestring, at the price of 3,000 of his soldiers' lives, he had caused the great showpiece, reputed bastion of imperial British power in Asia, to fall within seventy days of the start of hostilites. Expensive British roads and cheap Japanese bicycles had done it. He had not depended on lorries and trucks that could break down, catch fire, get jammed in bottlenecks or halted by road blocks. His total casualty list was less than ten thousand. The British had just experienced the greatest military disaster in their history. The whole glittering prize was Japan's within ten weeks. "Thank you very much, you have done a good job," he told his staff. "Now you can all drink as much saki as you like."

from Out in the Midday Sun, *Kate Caffery, Andre Deutsch Ltd, 1973*

JAPANESE DAYS
by Jacintha Abisheganaden

HERE is memory and history.

My mother is twelve. I see her with hair cropped short as a boy. Hiding above the latrine closet with her sister, my 'dragon aunt'. Hiding from the stranger. "They used to come in looking for the women."

The house is still there in Bukit Pasoh Road. Heart of Chinatown. Three storeys, dark and cool and smelling of wood and Chinese tea. Near the Millionaires Club. Ghosts under one staircase.

They tell me now that my grandmother painted her hair grey the morning the Japanese took Singapore. She was in her thirties.

There were Australian soldiers that passed that day.

"They were walking around like...like derelicts."

These are my grandfather's words.

We threw them tins of sardines and corned beef from the top floor as they passed. Nothing much to share."

"I went to the back of the house that morning and looked at the drain. No water. We had to ration because they said many people had been killed and the water was dirty. So don't take from the tap," my mother says.

"There was a stillness and smoke in the city. That was very scary. The silence. There had been a lot of bombing before they arrived. It was a smouldering city already."

"Mum", I say, "It was supposed to be Chinese New Year's day when the Japs came."

"I don't remember that. It was war."

I am a postwar baby and my imagination of the forties is culled and surely flawed by black and white MGM movies, by Glen Miller songs, by curry tiffin and cabaret girls.

Was there blood, mother, and does it stain a generation who can still remember?

Singapore, the prized naval base. Symbol of Western power in the Far East. A medal of prestige for the British.

Holding fort in 1941 was one Chief Staff Officer appointed to Malaya, a 'thin, delicate looking, bucktoothed' Lieutenant-Colonel, Arthur Ernest Percival.

On the last day of peace in Malaya, December 8th, Percival placed a call to Sir Thomas Shenton, the Governor of the Straits Settlements. It was a quarter past one in the morning. The Japanese had landed. They had opened fire. They had silenced the British pillboxes at Kota Bahru. Getting out of bed to answer the call, Thomas roared:

"Well I suppose you'll shove the little men off."

'The little men', 'The Yellow Peril', call them what you will, had been grossly underestimated by the British and this misunderstanding and error in judgement now goes down in history as testimony to an inevitable course of events.

At 4 o'clock that same morning, enemy aircraft were approaching Singapore twenty five miles away. The air raid sirens started to wail. From the dock area and the centre of town, the bombs exploded amidst the drone of the bombers.

The waterfront began to gather with people, mostly Chinese and Malay who along with some officials thought the whole thing was a practice alert.

Most of the bombs had fallen in Chinatown. Sixty-one people had been killed and a hundred and thirty-three injured.

This is the story of Francis A. Rodrigues, a customs officer who is 77 today and retired. The night those first bombs dropped on Singapore he was on the midnight shift at Keppel Road.

I interview Mr Rodrigues in the verandah of a terrace house in Katong which was near the sea at wartime. Now there is Marine Parade. We smoke cigarettes and drink soya bean out of tetrapacks. He wears a singlet with shorts and his hair is silver. A handsome Eurasian gent who has loved these stories and tells them lovingly.

"I went to church with my wife that morning. It was the Feast of Immaculate Conception. December 8th, 6.30 a.m. mass. We were living in government quarters in Keppel Road at the time.

"I was doing ARP (Air Raid Precautions) duty that night and at about 3 a.m. I think, the bombs dropped. I remember one of the bombs dropped behind our quarters. We were all scared and heard the drone of the bombers — 'woong woong woong', then the bomb.

"It came as a shock to everybody. They were preparing because we had formed ARP — people were told not to have any lights exposed outside their houses and all this. But that night, the whole of Singapore was lit up — the streets, everything.

"I can tell you I was drawing about $150 then. I could support a family of five children. I couldn't afford a car but there was a traction company running — we had electric trams and mosquito buses — they used to carry about 8 passengers. I remember the cinemas — Capitol and Cathay. They used to show Western epics

— Robert Taylor in *Quo Vadis*. About 40 cents a ticket.

"I was later recalled to my job during the Occupation after being jobless for a year. They paid me $100 Japanese dollars. It was worth a packet of Kooa cigarettes. During that year when I had no job we lived off my savings. But my wife and mother-in-law used to make oil out of coconuts and we would sell the bottles to friends — about 60, 70 cents.

"A lot of the Chinese were massacred. But there was a gentleman by the name of Shinozaki. He was very nice man, a good man and I suppose he had a soft spot for the Eurasians. He had been a civilian who was Japanese Intelligence before the War. Shinozaki worked out a plan with another man, Dr Charlie Paglar to resettle the Eurasians in Bahau (Negri Sembilan). It was actually jungle.

"They had to clean it up and build their own huts there. Medical supplies were not very good. There were many deaths from malaria and disease. I was asked to go but I was just recalled to my job working in the customs for the Japs."

"I remember not long after they occupied Singapore, there were a lot of heads hung on poles, placed on prominent roads.

"Indonesian heads on Orchard Road. They had been caught pilfering from the godowns."

"I expected terrible forfeits in the East," wrote Winston Churchill, "But all this would be merely a passing phase."

The shadow of the Second World War had not yet crossed Malaya even two years into the war. Arthur Ernest Percival counted his forces and asked for more — forty-eight more battalions. While he waited for his reply from London, the Japanese were systematically preparing themselves. In November 1941 they had in fact an army of over a million strong.

117

While the citizens of Singapore thought there were plenty of planes that the Allies had for Malaya, the records now show that the figure was clearly under 200.

In fact, in November 1941, there were only a few in Singapore who were wary.

Every Saturday morning the sirens were tested and every night the white searchlights arched over water. If you looked up there seemed to be many planes flying overhead and the country was "stiff with British and Australian troops" with promises of more to come.

So this became the stuff which made Singapore feel immune. She was Britain's biggest forfeit and she was had in an era altogether longer than a "a passing phase".

"While in terms of a nation's history, a period of three and a half years is merely a bad afternoon, memories as well as the gains after the war were long term."

These are my uncle's words. He will tell you about the memory:

"My elder brother Gerard Mathuram was sent away. He never returned."

The gains were more insidious. What finally emerged from the Occupation was a deep desire for national independence.

I love the sound of the "Liberty Cabaret". I think of a bar with beaded curtains where the patrons dance about chanting "Merdeka!" How strange and wonderful that it was here in North Bridge Road, at the Liberty Cabaret that the first political party after the war was born. The Malayan Democratic Union.

But we are here again in November 1941, before the carnage, before the slow shock of a fast approaching war where we meet Lieutenant General Tomoyuki Yamashita who when given orders to attack Singapore, was offered five divisions to do this with.

"No," replied the General, "Four will be enough."

My Chinese grandfather (my mother's father) is blind in one eye. He has suffered from a hernia for as long as I've been able to understand what it means. He used to race cars. The real thing. He used to build them out of scrap metal and spare parts and sell them after the war. During the Occupation when you could meet with certain death and unspeakable punishments for holding on to a radio, he stowed away and listened to a shortwave radio "with 21 valves."

No one will tell me exactly why he was caught, interrogated and jailed by the Japanese at the YMCA Kempetei headquarters.

He will tell me silly things like how the sentry guard that first day of detainment "fancied my watch and took it away."

He did tell me that while he was in jail he could hear men in the

next room being beheaded. He would first hear the begging, no, the pleading, then the "swish of the sword."

I like his machismo because he is a survivor. But I like his aeroplanes stories better.

One day in Prison:

"You can hear the buffalo bombers. They could go at 200 mph. The air raid siren comes, then you see the bombers and you're a dead duck, man.

"There were B-29's at 30,000 feet and then below them, the Jap Zero fighters (the lightest fastest single-seater) 10,000 feet below. I could hear the canon pumping out. The Zero planes run like mad. Very wonderful this B-29. All the prisoners and I were clapping."

All the time, Wong Loon Cheong is half laughing as he tells the stories; his good eye bright and beady.

February 15 1942. 11 a.m.

In a house in Florence Road, Upper Serangoon, my father who was then fifteen, greeted the Japanese soldiers who stopped there on bicycles with the only word he knew in Japanese.

He bowed from the waist and repeated 'Sayonara'.

"There were two soldiers wearing tight fitting khaki uniforms with hats which had flaps behind their necks. They had bayonets tied to their belts and no matter what they said it sounded aggressive.

"Miruku", they demanded (milk) and we gave them tins of condensed milk. The women in the house were hiding. They took away our bicycle. It was a Raleigh Rudge.

"My job then in the family was to maintain a trench with steps that were dug into the garden. I was very happy looking after this trench. I made a special hole beside it to keep water and biscuits for the air raids.

"I would have just left school when the war started. When the town was bombed, my father had decided that we should move from the house there to the 'country-side'.

"Much later I was laughing at the thought that my first words to the Japanese were 'good-bye'."

SINGAPORE SLING

How many more stories, — of your aunt or mine who baked cakes out of water and tapioca flour and little else. Of meals for whole families of cold tea mixed with rice. Of my father's brother who peddled gold at a stall next to Lee Kuan Yew's at a night market called Robinson Petang. ("Get this properly verified", I am told), of families who were cheated out of thousands of dollars when they sold their homes and possessions for banana money.

Of a world and a time one can never eradicate from the memory or history of our country.

As a country made up of immigrants, those who were to become Singaporeans had been governed by both Western and now Eastern powers. What was born after Japanese Surrender in 1945 was a fierce determination to come into our own.

In the words of our Prime Minister:

"My colleagues and I are of that generation of young men who went through the Second World War and the Japanese Occupation and emerged determined that no one — neither the Japanese nor the British — had the right to push and kick us around. We are determined that we could govern ourselves and bring up our children in a country where we can be proud to be self-respecting people...

"The scales had fallen from our eyes and we saw for ourselves that the local people could run the country."

RAFFLES:
THE MAGIC OF A NAME
by Raymond Flower

JUST a hundred years ago this month, when Orchard Road ran through orchards and a Mr Scott grew his fruit trees where Scott's Road joins it now (Mr Scott, by the way, was a relative of Sir Walter and a business associate of Francis Light, who founded Penang), two Armenian brothers alighted at Collyer Quay.

They already had a couple of hotels in Penang — the Eastern and the Oriental — which were subsequently amalgamated into the famous E & O. But they were also having trouble, for their landlord had suddenly decided to double the rent. I can't vouch for the story, of course, but one gathers that they shrugged their shoulders, saying that if this was his game they would pack their bags and move to Singapore instead. Presumably this counter-ploy worked, since the E & O continued to flourish in their hands. However, I suspect that, having tasted success in Penang, they had already decided to have a go in this bigger, more challenging market. At any rate here they were in April 1886, with the intention of opening a luxurious hotel.

Their carriage clip-clopped round the Cricket Club, then little more than a wooden pavilion, and along the Padang. They passed the Hotel de l'Europe, which stood in pillared splendour where the Supreme Court is today, skirted the Raffles Institution, now the site of Raffles City, and alighted at a bungalow on the corner of Bras Basah and Beach Road. In those days the sea still lapped the gardens of the mansions that fronted Beach Road, most of which were built in the colonial style and included a separate building with a billiard table inside. Very posh they were too. Their lofty white pillars and colonnades were lit up at night by brilliant silver lamps, and the stillness was only broken by the gentle ripple of the wavelets, a commentator wrote. One could easily imagine oneself, he thought "amid the garden palaces of the Arabian Nights."

The mansion on the corner belonged to a George Dare, who had come to grief financially through some unwise speculations. And so, having an excellent cook, he had turned his billiard room annexe into a tiffin room — a luncheon club, if you like. Certainly his lunches were the best in town, and you could eat in the garden among the chattering mynah birds. Seated at a table shaded by scarlet flame trees, with a view over the sea through the Travellers' palms, Martin and Tigran Sarkies knew immediately that this was the place for their hotel. ("That corner of the world smiles for me more than anywhere else" murmurs Martin, being well up with his Horace. "Spot on" replies Tigran.)

So negotiations were opened, and closed — as the saying goes — on 13 May 1886, leaving the Sarkies in possession of both the tiffin room and the mansion, which was being used as a girls' school. Once the girls

The original facade of Raffles Hotel

Raffles Hotel — Singapore.

123

had been moved elsewhere, the premises were spruced up and enlarged, causing some speculation in the local press. What would the new establishment be called? Clearly the matter of name is of vital importance to a hotel. It should be strong, or sincere, and preferably striking. Regent is great, for instance, if you happen to have a wonky monarch around, but less so in a republic. And, though it may be tactless to mention it, have you ever considered the last two syllables of Dynasty?

In this case the choice was obvious, given that the place was already known as the Raffles Girls' School and was slap across the road from the Raffles Institution and in sight of Sir Stamford's new statue in the middle of the Padang. But it was a final touch of artistry all the same. And so Raffles Hotel, which Noel Barber considers to be the most nostalgically named hostelry in the world, opened its doors on 1 December 1887. Before long it was to become affectionately known, in every corner of the globe, quite simply as "Raffles". (Not The Raffles, please — which sounds like a jumble sale.)

Ho! you say, noting the date, how come the centenary is being celebrated in this year of the tiger? The answer is simply that the Sarkies brothers kicked off, as it were, by operating the tiffin room. That was the actual birth of Raffles — a bit embryonic, to be sure, but only a nit-picker would insinuate that Singapore is at it again, doing the century in 99 years.

Be this as it may, one of the first guests was Joseph Conrad, who wrote of "the straggling building of bricks, as airy as a birdcage, the lofty rooms, the draughty corridors, the long chairs on the verandah," and described how periodic invasions from a passenger streamer "flitted through the wind-swept dusk of the apartments." Though he didn't mention the hotel by name (Conrad was never explicit about such things) it certainly sounds like Raffles in the 1880s.

Other accounts from that period speak of Raffles as a delightfully sunshaded, courtyarded, loose-limbed place, already famous for its food and cool drinks at the long teak bar with great glass mirrors behind. From this convivial haunt, we are told, emerged "corpulent Dutch visitors from Java, accompanied by bouncing Dutch ladies whose shrill laughs rent the air," while parties of tall Germans "strode along with military jaunt, enveloped in clouds of cigar smoke." A lady travelling on the Duke of Sutherland's yacht remembers cooling off on the verandah after a curry tiffin and watching some young English officers, who were leap-frogging round the billiard tables.

This was about the time that Rudyard Kipling wrote: "Providence conducted me along a beach, in full view of five miles of shipping — five solid miles of masts and funnels — to a place called Raffles Hotel, where the food is excellent as the rooms are bad. Let the traveller take note. Feed at Raffles and sleep at the Hotel de l'Europe."

As publishers sometimes do with book reviews, Tigran Sarkies extracted the words "Feed at Raffles, where the food is excellent" but omitted the bit about the rooms being bad. However he knew it was true. After all, they had previously been used as school dormitories. And so he set about buying up the adjoining properties (one of which was the American Consulate) and began erecting a splendid French Renaissance style building on the site of George Dare's old mansion. On 18 November 1899 the familiar shape of Raffles as we know it today was finally unveiled. The Palm Court cloisters followed a few years later.

The new building was so grand and swanky that Raffles soon became a byword in the vocabulary of travel. Its lofty dining room, still called the Tiffin Room, was the largest in the East. Its hundred apartments were all suites, each complete with sitting room, bedroom, bathroom and dressing-room. Palm trees lined the garden; there were tennis courts, livery stables, a private laundry, a dark room for amateur photographers, and even rubber-tyred jinrickshas.

Soon Sultans, royalty and business tycoons had become its regular guests along with rubber planters and sea captains who traded tall stories at the bar. The London Sphere called Raffles "The Savoy of Singapore" and Senator Stainiforth Smith of the US declared that "Raffles Hotel is more than a hostelry. It is an institution."

It soon became a favourite haunt for writers too. "I like Singapore better this time" observed Hermann Hesse during his visit in 1911, "We are staying expensively but well at Raffles" — a bland enough endoresment to be sure, but acceptable from the pen of a future Nobel Prize winner. Somerset Maugham, who wrote some of his stories in the garden (though not quite as many as is sometimes suggested) provided what must be the ultimate in quotes when he stated effusively that "Raffles stands for all the fables of the exotic East." Good old Willy! He may not have been popular with the colonial British, whose undisguised foibles formed the basis for several mordant tales, but at Raffles his memory will always be cherished.

In 1920 Arshak Sarkies, the youngest of the founding brothers, expanded the hotel further. Unfortunately, since no further land was available, it meant that some incongruous structures were erected around the main building. Along with a larger reception area and a new Long Bar, the great verandah facing the sea was covered over to form a new ballroom. Although this spoilt the facade, its spaciousness and airiness made it the most popular venue in all Singapore. From then on, the grandest balls were all held at Raffles.

Above all, the 1920s are associated with Maugham and Coward, with Charlie Chaplin, Frank Buck, and other movie stars such as Ronald Coleman, Jeanette MacDonald, Jean Harlow and Douglas Fairbanks heading what was surely an all-star cast.

Though Frank Buck left his cargo of wild animals at Johore, he stayed so long at Raffles and featured Singapore so prominently in his Bring 'em Back Alive films that he came to be regarded as an honorary citizen. Douglas Fairbanks and Mary Pickford were then, of course, the leaders of Hollywood society. Impeccably attired, they lunched in the Grill or at Government House. But one evening Fairbanks bet an athletic New Zealander that he could not hurdle over every table in the ballroom without tipping a glass. The Kiwi, togged out in tails, proceeded to do just that — ending up face first in the arms of the the band.

Noel Coward　　　　　　　　*Somerset Maugham*

Charlie Chaplin is remembered at Raffles as being a quiet, modest sort of chap, always dressed in a sober grey suit and not given to clowning at all. Yet when the little tramp with the bowler hat and stick arrived, he received a standing ovation from the normally torpid ricksha men — in contrast to Jean Harlow, whose pictures (like those of Mae West) had been so sternly censored that the Singapore public was hardly alert to her charms.

On his first visit, Noel Coward was greeted neither by mad dogs nor Englishmen out in the midday sun, but by a ferocious tropical thunderstorm. Sitting on the verandah sipping a gin sling and staring at the muddy sea, he felt as though he were "inside a hot cardboard box which was growing rapidly smaller and smaller." But this did not stop him from staying for a month, during which he sportingly took part in a production of R.C. Sheriff's *Journey's End* that was being put on at the Victoria Theatre. Since he had previously turned down the lead in

127

SINGAPORE SLING

America, it gave Singapore the chance to see a spectacle that Broadway was denied. In three days he learnt the lines, and gave such a sensational performance in this moving play that both critics and audiences were entranced.

But his offstage antics with members of the cast caused some eyebrows to be raised. "Some of the more refined socialites of Singapore looked obliquely at us, as if we were not quite the thing" he admitted, "a little too rowdy perhaps, on the common side. I'm sure they were right. Actors always laugh more loudly than other people when they're enjoying themselves, and we laughed most of the time."

The Governor's wife certainly didn't laugh when he arrived late for dinner. But having been soundly ticked off by Lady Clementi, Coward got his own back by staging a West End comedy set in a colonial Government House with a hit refrain entitled *"Menenti, Menenti"* ("Wait, Wait"). Since Lady C. was by no means popular, this caused considerable glee in the colony.

Needless to say, the eccentrics are those who tend to be remembered most. If Noel Coward's silk monogrammed shirts and blue beret stood out in the fashionable crowd at Raffles, the gargantuan bulk of the archaeologist Callenfels — immortalized by Conan Doyle as Professor Challenger — was even more conspicuous. Heaving and shuddering like a shaken blancmange in his curry-stained pyjamas, he lectured to anyone who cared to listen in a voice that could be heard on the other side of the Palm Court. He was said to have consumed ten bottles of gin for breakfast, and regularly put away 30 bottles of beer at a sitting. Nor was his capacity for food any less remarkable. Once, for a bet, he ate every dish on the hotel menu — and then went through the menu again in reverse order, just to show that he could do it.

Behind these exotic folk loomed the hospitable presence of Arshak Sarkies, whose favourite party trick was to waltz around the ballroom balancing a full glass of whisky on his bald head. Yet Arshak's worldliness concealed an incredibly generous heart, and in his later days it was said that he ran both the E & O and Raffles more for the pleasure of entertaining his friends than to make money. But sadly, this open-handedness led to the collapse of his business empire after the stock market crash of 1929.

In 1933 Raffles was reconstituted as a public company, and for the first time this quintessentially British hotel became largely British owned, though it was run by a Swiss manager. By then the Hotel de l'Europe had been torn down to make way for the Supreme Court, and in the heady years before World War II, when Malaya was producing nearly half the world's output of tin and rubber, and Singapore was becoming a formidable naval and military base, Raffles must have seemed an embodiment of the British Raj. Though Singapore itself was a city of extravagant contrasts, life in the hotel was conducted in the truest colonial tradition. If anyone went on to the dance floor without being attired in full evening dress, the orchestra stopped playing and the offender was asked to leave. With the exception of visiting dignitaries and some Babas, few Asians stayed at Raffles during this colour-conscious period of the Empire.

However Mr Nakajima, who operated a photo shop in the Raffles arcade, was assiduously taking pictures of the high-ranking British officers who frequented the hotel and other compatriots of his were not wasting their time either. We all know why.

Yet even as the Japanese army was slicing down the Malay Peninsula like a knife through butter, life at Raffles carried on as normal. English ladies took their tea, and the Long Bar was crammed with officers and tuans downing their gin slings and stengahs. Though the ballroom was blacked-out, air raids were regarded as a tiresome interruption to social activities. Indeed despite the appalling bombardments just before the fall of Singapore, Raffles continued to dance on until the end — and emerged unscathed. You see, the bombers had been ordered to make sure not to hit it. The Japanese had their own plans for Raffles.

Renamed "Syonan Ryokan" it was commandered for the use of VIPs, and bemused room-boys who were used to British spit and polish had to cope with half naked samurai whirling swords round their heads. They soon learnt to bow deeply to all Japanese guests under the pain of a sharp slap on the face if they didn't incline deeply enough. However the staff did at least manage to save some of the hotel's treasures. The magnificent silver roast beef trolley was buried in the Palm Court and, despite all the invaders' attempts to find it, remained undetected throughout the Occupation.

Immediately after the war Raffles was used as a rehabilitation centre for hundreds of refugees from Java and the East Indies. In 1946 it opened its doors to the public again, more or less as before but a bit less (if I may paraphrase a well-known slogan). Yet if the atmosphere, like the whole colonial way of life, was perceptably changing, Raffles remained the best address in Southeast Asia, and continued to be a magnet for the rich and the famous.

Once again the social graces thrived against a background of fashion shows and fancy dress balls. To the music of Xavier Cugat's orchestra, people jumped into fountains in evening dress, while planters and officers exchanged stories about the Emergency and the fighting that was going on just over the Causeway. Celebrated names such as Pandit Nehru, Emperor Haile Selassie, Premier Sato, President Saragat of Italy and Pierre Trudeau of Canada studded the hotel registers. When Prince Faisal of Saudi Arabia came in 1955, extra suites had to be improvised for his five-day visit by knocking down some walls. And slap in the middle of a function that was being given in her honour, Elizabeth Taylor's gown suddenly fell to bits, exposing more of her splendid body than Liz had intended.

Yet in the 1950s, when Tan Chin Tuan bought control of Raffles, its tropical sunset seemed to be approaching as Independence loomed. The hotel was then considered to be a discriminating, colonial relic. Not only did it occupy a highly desirable piece of estate but, worse still, it was losing money. While glossy new hotels were shooting up all around Orchard Road, Raffles appeared to be stagnating. There was talk of rebuilding the hotel along the coast by the Swimming Club. Indeed when Roberto Pregarz took over the management some 19 years ago, his predecessor told him: "Good luck! They will close the place in six months."

Instead, the grand old lady of Beach Road was saved, not just by a world outcry, but by the desire of many Singaporeans to preserve a priceless national heritage. And they were right. For once the truth sank in that it is precisely in its past that the hotel's future lies, Raffles went from strength to strength. Three years ago, the building was officially listed as an historic landmark by the Monument Preservation Board, and plans are afoot to restore the place to its Belle Epoque splendour.

It may not be the most modern or the most luxurious hotel in

Singapore today, but it is still one of the half dozen most famous hotels in the world. Australians love it. Americans cherish it. Japanese photograph it. The BBC centred one of their most successful television series, "Tenko" around Raffles and are planning a sequel. Australia's Ray Martin Show featured Raffles twice in 1985, and hardly a day passes without an article about the hotel appearing somewhere around the globe.

When the QE2 was in town last spring two sportsmen from BBC flew out from London on Concorde to have a Singapore Sling at Raffles, and then they flew back home in the afternoon. That's twenty thousand kilometres for a couple of drinks!

Why do they choose Raffles, you ask? Well in part it is nostalgia, of course. The romance of this famous place whose name Philip Morris have adopted for their new best-selling brand of cigarette. But is also a question of atmosphere.

You sense the ambience as soon as you walk in. It is made up of all sorts of things: tradition, homeliness, the friendliness of the staff. The magic of sitting in the Palm Court at dusk as the orchestra plays the lilting melodies of Gershwin or Strauss, of walking from your suite straight out into a tropical garden, of kippers for breakfast to the music of the songbirds, of meeting faces you haven't seen for years as you relax by the pool.

Equally, it's a question of character — the character by which the greatness of the city itself can be judged.

In the century to come Raffles has a special part to play in Singapore. And though we shall all be getting pretty long in the tooth by 2086, I give you a toast to its bicentenary!

The True Story
of the Origins of
an Unnamed Singapore
Corporation
by Hugh Mabbett

IN the old days you could get by in Singapore just by being white. There were a lot of pompous asses about — white, of course — who really believed they were a superior breed, and a lot more, officer types, pining for chaps they could order around, like they did in the war. You learned to play the game their way and, bingo, you were in — job, car, a little house in Serangoon Garden, clubs, money left over for drinking and whoring. Easy.

So choosing to get demobbed from the army in Singapore after the Japanese war, rather than being sent back to Scotland, turned out well. I worked in an engineering place for a while, then I was a kind of fixer down at the docks, and for a long time I was with the old Singapore Traction Company. Remember the STC? I knew bugger all about buses, so perhaps I was the reason it ran into strife and the government had to take over. I was a pretty expert fiddler by this time, making money on the side. You could not get away with it now, but in those days everyone was on the take.

The main thing was to be a good chap — good war record, even if you made it up yourself, good drinker, plenty of dirty stories — and I played that line for all it was worth. They were good years. But as time went by the line got shorter. People who had become managers or whatever on the strength of family connections or through an old boy network faded away and a more miserable lot came in, men with beady eyes and rat-trap mouths and balance-sheet brains; jumped-up book-keepers. They didn't give a shit that I spoke fair Hokkien and Malay and knew how bribery worked and was popular in every brothel in Lavender Street. These fellows were a pain in the arse.

Their idea of giving visiting directors from England a good time was a boring evening in the Tanglin Club when all the poor sods wanted, all they had finangled the whole trip for, was an exotic lay. Instead, they were kept talking shop for hours, port and cigars and all that, till even the cheapest whorehouses had packed up for the night. I would catch their eyes across the table — I would be there as the company's expert on local politics, so help me — and see them pleading for release, I hated these evenings as much as the visitors did.

Perhaps I made my discontent too obvious. I was no longer such a good chap, and jobs began drying up. Inevitable, I suppose, because these new types soon worked out that local people could do the sort of jobs I had had for much less. I ran downhill pretty fast and I wondered if I would ever be able to bounce up again. I wondered about this even more when the only job I could get was as driver to a Chinese stockbroker.

He was delighted to have me, along with his Mercedes and his diamond-studded watch and his hideaway flats and his hideaway mistresses. Some of it was good. He would take me drinking and whoring with him, and would even take over the driving when I was drunk, snoring away in the back seat. But then he would have me waiting for hours outside the Cricket Club, with all the other drivers. Sod this for a lark, I thought, remembering the days when I had had drivers of my own. I perceived a crisis in my life, you might say. It was time I did something to get back into that club, and all the others.

One way would have been to marry a rich woman, but do you have any ideas how closely the wealthy people of Singapore guarded their daughters in those days? Especially from white trash? Some fellows managed it but you had to be lucky, and not a British Other Ranker whose career did not really stand examination. There had to be another way. I found it too, in a flash of inspiration that came to me at the Singapore railway station one night.

I was seeing friends off on the Express to Kuala Lumpur. The Malayan Emergency was on and there were a lot of military people about. The train had a pretty luxurious first class, and the rest of it was fair enough — except for a kind of cattle truck right on the back, with wooden benches and broken windows. It was labelled, For British Other Ranks Only. The officers were up in the first class with their wine and whisky, while the men who did the work were being treated like scum. That sign brought a flash of inspiration. I had been a British Other Rank. I knew how lousy their lives were — hard, hot, no money, no respect. I knew how much a little extra money could mean to them. Over the next couple of weeks I shopped around among the lads. I had been one of them and we spoke the same language, and I soon found some willing to have a go at whatever I might devise.

Now, two points. First, this true story is being written because I owe a favour. I would sooner not write it but for reasons I cannot go into I must. It is something to do with an obligation to an old colleague; work it out for yourself. Second, because this is a true story, and because some Singapore people now in remarkably high positions are involved, I shall skip many details, and change some, and just give you the bare bones anyway. One detail I have changed is my name. Life is too good now to let myself get involved in a scandal, even if it is more than twenty years old. The name I have used? I made it up — no one could have a name like that, so it is safe enough. On with the story.

Well, I had worked out that all those unhappy British Other Ranks, mostly conscripted national servicemen fighting a war they could not care less about, were splendidly placed to help run any operation I might invent. Then I made another discovery. There used to be a lot more pet shops around Selegie Road than there are today, and I had become friendly with some of their owners. One day, one of them told me a tiny bird he had was worth forty pounds in England. Forty quid! A lot of money in those days, just for a creature smaller than the palm of my hand. "Tropical birds — big business," my friends said, and that was it.

Within a couple of months we had a bloody marvellous operation going. There were Royal Air Force planes going from Changi to

England all the time, and the national servicemen out there were just as well disposed to picking up a bit of extra cash as the army boys were. We would buy up birds all over Singapore, pack them, and ship them off to high-ranking people all over England, complete with every document you might think of. We even had plane crews looking after our birds during the flight. Then, at the other end (anything is easy if you have good people in the right places) the boxes would be diverted, as it were, and the dealers would pay up and take over.

It got better. Our buying in Singapore pushed up prices so we began going right to the source, right into the swamps and jungles to catch our own birds. You think that all those patrols out in Malaya and Borneo were looking for the enemy? Some, maybe, but not all — some were becoming the best bring 'em back alive experts in the business. You cannot begin to imagine the exotic specimens we fed into our pipeline. Hornbills from Sarawak were especially good business, and not all that difficult to trap; or perhaps we would buy pet ones from the Ibans.

You would like to know what else we sent? I have just been looking through Glenister's book on the birds of the Malay peninsula and Smythies' book on the birds of Borneo. There is hardly one we did not deal in at some stage, and some we dealt with in hundreds. Orioles, kingfishers, sunbirds, drongos, magpie robins, merboks and sharmas and so on and so forth. Some officers were puzzled by men who so suddenly switched from knowing nothing about anything to being eager ornithologists, and some wanted to know why men were carrying mist nets into the jungle. "To catch fish in the streams," was the usual answer. Officers will believe anything if it is silly enough.

There were some dicey moments at Changi with officious bastards wanting to know more about these boxes getting such special attention. But in general any squaddie is a match for any officer, especially as we were careful to give every box an impressive set of papers as well as an impressive address. Some appeared to be the personal property of very senior officers and diplomats, and I was especially pleased with those we labelled as if they were going to military research stations with

'Secret' printed all over them.

A couple of majors caught on, but as our people knew they were shipping stuff home which they should not, they were in no position to make a fuss. Then we captured a colonel, caught him cold doing that which he should not have done, and we had protection in high places as well. All this meant that officers were not that much of a problem. Their own system made them very vulnerable. Few of them got enough money to live the way they expected to live, with all their clubbing and entertaining, so fifty quid here and there could work magic. It would pay an overdue bar bill, or get the car fixed, or buy a wife the kind of dress she thought she needed to wear when meeting the colonel's lady. In fact, some wives became our most useful allies within the system. I came to feel sorry for some of the officers, trying to carry on as if the world had not changed in ways beyond their comprehension.

There were a few hiccups. Some of the local dealers tried to cut themselves in, but what is the point of having big, strong military policemen around if you do not use them? It was the same at the other end. If any dealer got bright ideas about shaking us down, there would be a knock on his door in the middle of the night and a couple of our tall lads standing there to help him see reason. The trade in general did not know what to do except go along with us. We were unfair competition, in a way, and the big dealers hated us, but on the other hand we helped a lot of small operators make money. Back in Singapore we brought in a couple of local dealers who knew the business and had Secret Society connections, just as insurance. And we made a lot of money.

It was all so easy. Or perhaps easy is the wrong word — perhaps 'obvious' would be better. We got the birds cheap, transport was free, cash was on delivery; none of us even paid income tax. After a time we began to see that though we had covered all obvious angles it was all too good to last. It was time to think of the future. We had a meeting at the old Chequers Hotel, where officers used to take other officers' wives to talk things over. There were eight of us — me, three army, two airforce, and two local men, now very well known, who would be most aggrieved today if they should be publicly connected with our shenanigans.

All went well at first. We agreed that the bird trade, however good it had been to us, was not a permanent way of life. The British would be moving their forces out of Singapore before long and the international movement to protect wildlife was getting stronger each year. At the local level, even as small a thing as a new security chief at customs could put us in strife. We agreed to start running the business down, paying off everyone and clearing the decks, as it were, while we looked for something else to do.

What would that be? That was when the meeting got rough. Four of the men there argued that we could put our expertise to work in more lucrative ways — "Birds are for the bird," one said, forgetting how much money birds had made him. They were all for guns and drugs, and that is the way they went, on their own. Two of the four were dead within two years, another is serving a life prison sentence in a place where you would not want to remain overnight, and the fourth is getting along as best he can without the eyes and hands he left behind in the mountains of Vietnam when a business trip turned sour.

As for the rest of us, perhaps we were not really criminals at heart. Smuggling birds was a kind of victimless crime. No one got hurt, people got what they wanted, and even the birds were as well looked after as we could manage. We actually cared for them, unlike the bird smugglers today who expect huge death rates and make their money out of the survivors. Guns and drugs were not the same thing. I suppose we were all frightened of big time crime, as well. We calculated that we had enough money between us to go legitimate, and we did, and we could not have made a better decision.

The small investment company we set up has been through a couple of name changes, the better to protect our origins, and its title now is a household word throughout Singapore. Do not try to work out which one it is, though, for you will never succeed. We have covered our tracks very thoroughly.

All you need to know is that I am back in all the clubs, though I hardly ever visit them, they are such boring places. Life is pretty good. My three colleagues also live so well that the past, when we think about it, which is not often, seems like a dream. On the other hand, if we ever get around to writing our formal company history, that story will have to be a dream, a public relations exercise dreamt up to conceal the truth. Perhaps there are skeletons in the backgrounds of all our big companies; perhaps that is why so few of them ever tell the story of their origins; perhaps they are basically as disreputable as us.

I mean, who would believe that our huge operation today, employing so many people, so useful to the economy of Singapore, was born illegally out of bird smuggling? At times, as I sit in my Rolls while my English driver — the only one in Singapore, as I am told — takes me here and there, I have trouble believing it myself.

CHINESE
MEDICINE MEN
by Sit Yin Fong

MANY a Western doctor might well shudder at Chinese cures for sickness and disease that are still practised in Singapore today.

Chinese medical practice is often crude. It is weird, superstition-laden, completely unscientific, and borders on black magic.

Here are a few of the strange beliefs in the remedial properties of animals taken as food.

Let's start with toothache. If you dread the dentist, then your man is a priest-doctor, or even the head of your family if he has picked up the particular Chinese art of healing toothaches without pincers.

The healer simply hammers a nail into the floor boards, muttering some incantations and your toothache is gone. In explanation, some folk hint vaguely at hypnotism. Others say it is auto-suggestion.

You can, of course, also cure toothache by tickling the inflamed tooth with a single tiger's whisker. Don't ask me how this comes about.

You've got a belly-ache? Well, there are many cures. One effective antidote is to drink a tea made from the dung of a certain grasshopper.

Suppose that is not handy. Then all you have to do is to get somebody to pinch the blood vessels in your back, near the shoulder blades, in the case of a slight attack. For a serious ailment, tackle the blood vessels under the armpits.

Your friend has got to know how to do it though. Else he might kill you by picking on the wrong blood vessels!

SINGAPORE SLING

It would seem from appearances that some parents of sick Chinese infants do not care about the existence of doctors or medicine.

The thought instantly jumps to their mind that the child has been frightened by malignant spirits and his "soul" has momentarily fled from his body.

The cure is the roadside prayer ritual, called the *kew keang* — in which an old woman chants to chasten the evil spirits and invite the "soul" home.

The next cure is for the attention of gourmets. Should a fish or chicken bone get stuck in your throat, don't panic and rush for the doctor. It won't be pleasant to face his mouth-jack and long pincers. Why not try this simple cure?

Sit tight while your quack writes four chinese characters on a slip of paper and stirs the paper in a cup of water. He mutters incantations, of course, and you drink the charmed liquid.

The four characters are *kow loong far hoi* meaning "the dragon disappears into the sea". Likewise, your troublesome bone disappears into thin air in the twinkling of an eye.

If you don't want to have anything to do with charms, there is an equally effective remedy.

Drink a tea prepared with water and burnt crab-shell ash, or the ash of the back-bone of the *Lei-yue* (carp).

In less time than it takes to tell, the bone in your throat melts away or is dislodged.

If a spider's web or some other mote gets into your eye, be very calm about it. Just keep on blowing bubbles into a cup of vinegar with a drinking straw until the foreign body is "transferred" to it.

Should a sty erupt on your eye, do nothing more than tie a black thread round the third finger of the hand opposite to the affected eye. The sty will quickly subside and give you peace, so it is claimed.

The Western scientific cure for goitre is to restore the iodine deficiency of a person's drinking water. The Chinese remedy is poles apart — and not without a touch of glamour.

SINGAPORE SLING

It is this: "Wear a pearl necklace". If the pearls are real ones, they are supposed to possess medical properties which can gradually reduce the swelling of the neck.

Or, if it is a magical cure you want for goitre, tie a bundle of charm papers to a tree. The transferring idea again!

So you have punctured your foot by stepping on the sharp point of a rusty nail. The first principle of modern first-aid is to cleanse the wound thoroughly and prevent dirt from getting into it. The object is to avoid blood-poisoning or gangrene.

The Chinese cure is different. They pick on the dirtiest or most evil-smelling foodstuff possible, *blachan*, or shrimp paste.

This is almost a poison because it has been exposed for weeks or months to the sun, dust and flies in the process of manufacture.

The paste is knocked into a flat cake, baked over an oven, slapped over the wound and securely bound up.

Believe it or not, the cure is 100 per cent infallible. You can almost see the rust and dirt sucked out of the wound by the *blachan*.

Chinese say the principle of this medical strategy is to "attack poison with poison". The *blachan* cure is also good for boils.

The poison versus poison principle is varied a little for the treatment of little boils in the region of the lips, considered to be the most dangerous of their kind because they are especially susceptible to blood poisoning.

In this case, grind a live poisonous spider with cooked rice and cover the boil with the paste.

For mending bone fractures, Chinese physicians insist that copper dust, filed from the ordinary copper coin, is an indispensable ingredient of the cure.

Live leeches pounded into a sticky paste are required to repair torn blood vessels or flesh tissue.

Mumps? Just paint the affected parts with washing blue.

Want hair to grow on your bald patches? Rub them with live flies.

The drinking of a child's urine is the last desperate measure to save the life of a person who has fallen from a height.

Live, new-born mice rank high as a Chinese medical panacea. There is said to be no better natural cure than mice for tuberculosis.

The crude way is to swallow alive several mice wrapped in the soft, sweet dried flesh of the *long ngan* fruit.

Connoisseurs roast the mice on a roof-tile over an open fire. They are then ground into powder and taken with brandy.

This nauseous concoction is believed to be an omnipotent body nourisher and aphrodisiac.

Apparently, Chinese physicians are reluctant to part with the mice cure for paralysis. A particularly good Chinese physician friend of mine only let out his so-called "secret" to me after much persuasion. This is his prescription.

Drown a dozen or so live mice in a bottle of old wine or brandy. Put the bottle away for at least one year. The resultant fermented liquid is said to be worth its weight in gold as a paralysis cure.

My friend said: "The stuff works like magic. A man may be bedridden for years. Take a little cup of it, and he will not only walk, but run."

There is one strict stipulation about the use of mice as medicine. The creatures must be blind as they were born. Their potency is lost once their eyes are open.

The catching of live mice provides what amounts to almost a livelihood for Chinatown urchins. Each mouse will fetch as much as 50 cents.

The ash of roasted mice is also good for cuts and bruises and the treatment of internal injuries. It is also an aphrodisiac.

Besides mice, there are other cures for T.B. A very old and revered Chinese practitioner of Western medicine, who is retired but still lives in Singapore today, always recommended dog meat and dog soup because he reasoned that dogs are seldom infected with this disease.

Dog's meat is, of course, also a remedy for malaria. The soup is a very potent and much sought-after aphrodisiac into the bargain.

Urchins make a business of providing the Chinese physician with the livestock which are his raw materials.

Great stress is laid on common cooking garlic as a natural cure for T.B. The humble herb may well yield hitherto unknown medical properties good for the lungs.

I would also recommend the doctors to look into the properties of two Malayan edible seeds — the *bua bua tai*, which are strung out like a belt of bullets, and their relation, the *bua chi ling* which are in pairs, and look like sun goggles.

These seeds, eaten as condiments mostly by Malays and Malayan Chinese *babas* and *nonyas*, smell horribly. But they are said to provide a 100 per cent cure for diabetes as well as absolute immunity from the complaint.

That is why, the Chinese say, Malays are seldom diabetic patients.

Another vegetable medicine is the dwarf onion which the Chinese call "fire onion". These are supposed to be able to cure dropsy but only if eaten in the right way.

Let the patient sit by an oven while the onions are being roasted over a roof-tile.

As each onion bursts with the heat, it should be snatched away and eaten immediately by the patient. He must eat until he is full. The onions will drive away the water from the patient's swollen body.

Ginger has its medicinal uses too. Its juice is prescribed for sunstroke and fainting fits.

Crocodile flesh is good for venereal diseases as well as coughs and asthma. It should be boiled with the Chinese herb *wai sang kok* and dried orange peel to take away the smell.

Cat soup is rated such a powerful body nourisher that the Chinese say, "Each helping gives you a 10-year span of new life."

Cat gourmets steam the cat meat with chicken, black beans, sugar cane and herbs for six or seven hours to get its full flavour.

They smack their lips and rave: "It's delicious. It gives you a cool feeling in the throat."

The cat must be old, however, something between 10 and 20 years of age. Young cats are useless. That is why it is hard or virtually impossible to find old cats in Chinatown. They are all eaten.

My physician friend said he recently spotted a very old cat in a shop in Temple Street. Every time he looked at the cat, there were about 10 other pairs of hungry human eyes following the movements of the supercilious creature as it sauntered out for a stroll.

Chinese kill a cat by hitting it on the head, after dosing it with brandy and making it drunk. The preparation of the meat can be a messy affair. You have to do it carefully. The fur won't come off once you let it touch the fat behind the creature's ears.

Said my friend: "Besides, killing a cat has to be a very secretive affair. It is against the law."

"Mischievous small boys have a way of finding out where you buried the head and guts, and dig them up. Then sanitary and what-not inspectors will come around making a lot of fuss."

Cat soup is also good for T.B.

Another physical restorer is tiger gelatin, extracted from the marrow of tiger bones which are steamed for one full month in a man-sized kitchen contraption.

This highly expensive stuff can be bought only by the *tahils* in Chinese drug shops. Tiger gelatin is the rejuvenator of the rich Chinese as cat soup is that of the poor.

Two favourite body stimulants for rich old Chinese are *yoong* (horn of deer), and *sam* (a rare plant found only in Korea and Japan).

These two things are revered almost as elixirs, and are among the most expensive items that money can buy in Chinese medicine. Wrapped in silk, they are sold in grammes.

The best *yoong* is that won from a deer while the animal is mortally wounded but still alive after a chase by its hunters. Such *yoong* is reckoned to contain life-giving properties as the blood and vital energy of the deer are said to rush up its horns during an exciting pursuit.

The *yoong* taken from a deer after it is dead is not so good.

The best *sam* is the wild species of the plant which is said to be difficult to find. The cultivated kind costs less.

SINGAPORE SLING

GINSENG

The "king of *sam*" called the *yan sam* (human *sam*) comes from a plant which closely resembles a man, with arms akimbo and legs outstretched.

Genuine pearls ground into powder are another of the most expensive items in Chinese medicine. They are administered to soothe children who have fallen sick through fright.

Chinese regard the gall as the organ which controls courage in both man and beast. Wild animals and reptiles are reckoned to be courageous, and therefore their galls are highly valued for medicinal purposes.

The galls of the tiger, bear and python are the most popular. Galls are dried in the sun until they become as hard as stone. They are good for many minor ailments, including sore eyes, boils and flesh sores, and are also used as a pain-killer.

Galls are sometimes eaten raw. I once saw a Chinese farmer rip open the belly of an iguana he had captured, made a grab for the gall and gulped this down, blood and all, without batting an eyelid.

He said he was fond of all kinds of animal galls because they gave him courage and also assured him good eye-sight in old age.

Such creatures as the turtle, shark, frog, earthworm, cockroach, snake and ant-eater are also found frequently in the Chinese pharmocopoeia.

The Chinese, therefore, must be counted among the most carnivorous people in the world. There are few creatures of the land, sea and air, wild or domesticated, in which the Chinese do not see value as either. food or medicine.

Big money is made by racketeer spiritualists in Singapore. The average Chinese calls on a medium if he is disappointed in love, wishes to vent a hatred, be cured of an illness, find a lost article, or get a job.

It isn't just a certain number of individuals who are involved but virtually the entire population.

And the money they pay all goes to swell the coffers of the spiritualist spivs.

At its low best, the racket is a shameless exploitation of superstition. The medium receives consultation fees for this phoney dabbling with the occult.

At the worst, it is extortion. The practitioner puts a gullible person in fear of some supposedly impending fate — unless so-much money is spent in prayers to appease such-and-such a deity ....

There are hundreds of spiritualist dens in Singapore and probably thousands in the Federation.

They do not operate in the open but clandestinely — partly to engender an appropriate air of mystery.

The business is carried on in a remote temple, a shophouse in an obscure street, or in some dank Chinatown cubicle.

from Tales of Chinatown by Sit Yin Fong, Heinemann Educational Books (Asia) Pte Ltd.

THE FOUNDING OF SINGAPORE
from The Malay Annals

HERE now is the story of a city called Palembang in the land of Andelas. It was ruled by Dĕmang Lebar Daun, a descendant of Raja Shulan, and its river was the Muara Tatang. In the upper reaches of the Muara Tatang was a river called the Mĕlayu, and on that river was a hill called Si-Guntang Mahameru. In that region lived two widows, Wan Ĕmpok and Wan Malini, and the two of them had planted padi on Bukit Si-Guntang. Much ground had they planted and their padi had thriven beyond words. When the padi was ripe over the whole field, it happened that one night Wan Ĕmpok and Wan Malini beheld from their house a glow as of fire on Bukit Si-Guntang. And they said, "Can that be the light of fire that glows yonder? It frightens me." Then said Wan Malini, "Whisht! It may be the gleam of the gem on some great dragon's head!" So Wan Ĕmpok and Wan Malini kept quiet in their fear and presently they fell asleep. When day dawned, Wan Ĕmpok and Wan Malini arose from their sleep and bathed their faces, and Wan Ĕmpok said to Wan Malini, "Come, let us go and see what it was that glowed like fire last night". Wan Malini agreed, and the two of them climbed up Bukit Si-Guntang, where they saw that their padi had golden grain, leaves of silver and stems of gold alloy. And when they saw what had happened to their padi, they said, "This is what we saw last night!" And as they walked along the hill they saw that the crest had turned into gold. According to one tradition it has a colour as of gold to this day. And on this land that had been turned into gold Wan Ĕmpok and Wan Malini beheld three youths of great beauty. All three of them were adorned like kings and wore crowns studded with precious stones, and they rode upon white elephants. Wan Ĕmpok and Wan Malini were lost in wonder and utterly amazed at the sight of these youths who were so handsome, bore themselves with such grace and were so brilliantly adorned. And they thought in their hearts, "Was it perchance because of these three youths that our padi has grain of gold, leaves of silver and stems of gold alloy and that this hilltop has been turned into gold?" And they asked the three youths, "Whence come you, sirs? Are you sons of genies or sons of fairies? For we have long been here without seeing anyone. Until you appeared today no human being has visited this place."

And the three youths made answer, "Not from the breed of genies or fairies are we. We are descended from Raja Iskandar Dzu'l-Karnain: of the lineage of Raja Nushirwan, Lord of the East and the West, are we." And Wan Empok and Wan Malini said, "What have you to prove the truth of what you say?" And the three youths answered, "These crowns that we wear are the sign: they shew that we are of the stock of Raja Iskandar Dzu'l-Karnain. If you doubt our word, the proof is that because we alighted on this spot your padi has grain of gold, leaves of silver and stems of gold alloy and this hilltop has been turned into gold." And Wan Empok and Wan Malini believed the words of the three young princes, and they were filled with joy and took the three young princes to their house. And the padi was reaped, and Wan Empok and Wan Malini became rich because of their meeting with the princes.

Now when the Raja of Palembang, whose name was Dĕmang Lebar Daun, had heard the story of how Wan Empok and Wan Malini had met with princes who had come down from heaven, he went to the house of Wan Empok and Wan Malini to see the princes, whom he then took back with him to the city. And it was noised over the whole country that descendants of Raja Iskandar Dzu'l-Karnain were now in Palembang, having come down from Bukit Si-Guntang Mahameru. Thereupon every ruler from every part of the country came to pay his respects to them. The eldest of the princes was taken by the people of Andelas to their country and was made Raja at Menangkabau, with the title of Sang Sapurba. Thereafter came the people of Tanjong Pura and took the second of the three princes to Tanjong Pura where they made him Raja with the title of Sang Maniaka, whilst the youngest of the three princes remained at Palembang with Demang Lebar Daun, who made him Raja of Palembang with the title of Sang Utama. Demang Lebar Daun thereupon abdicated and became chief minister.

Now Wan Empok and Wan Malini had a cow, silvery white in colour. And one day by the will of God this cow spewed foam from its mouth. From this foam came forth a human being called Bath. And Bath gave to Sang Utama the title of Sri Tri Buana. Sri Tri Buana became famous as a ruler; and all mankind, male and female, came from every part of the country to pay their homage to him, all of them bringing offerings for his acceptance. When Sri Tri Buana was established on the throne, he wished for a consort; and wherever there was to be found a beautiful daughter of a prince he took her to wife. But any such princess, when she slept with the king, was found by him the following morning to be stricken with chloasma as the result of being possessed by him, whereupon he abandoned her. To no less than thirty-nine princesses had this happened. Now it came to the king's ears that Dĕmang Lebar Daun had a daughter, Wan Sendari by name, whose beauty was such that she had no equal in those days. Sri Tri Buana asked Dĕmang Lebar Daun for her hand in marriage; but Dĕmang Lebar Daun replied, "If your Highness avails himself of your humble servant's daughter, she will assuredly be stricken with chloasma. But if your Highness desires your humble servant's daughter, then must your Majesty make a covenant with your humble servant, whereupon your humble servant will offer her for your Majesty's acceptance." And Sri Tri Buana asked, "What is this undertaking that you would have of me?" Demang Lebar Daun answered, "Your Highness, the descendants of your humble servant shall be the subjects of your Majesty's throne, but they must be well treated by your descendants. If they offend, they shall not, however grave be their offence, be disgraced or reviled with evil words: if their offence is grave, let them be put to death, if that is in accordance with Muhammadan law.

151

And the king replied, "I agree to give the undertaking for which you ask: but I in my turn require an undertaking from you, sir." And when Demang Lebar Daun asked what the undertaking was, the king answered, "that your descendants shall never for the rest of time be disloyal to my descendants, even if my descendants oppress them and behave evilly." And Demang Lebar Daun said, "Very well, your Highness. But if your descendants depart from the terms of the pact, then so will mine." And Sri Tri Buana replied, "Very well, I agree, I agree to that covenant": whereupon both of them took a solemn oath to the effect that whoever departed from the terms of the pact, let his house be overturned by Almighty God so that its roof be laid on the ground and its pillars be inverted.

When the covenant had been made and strict promises mutually given, Princess Wan Sendari was offered by Demang Lebar Daun to Sri Tri Buana, and Sri Tri Buana was wedded to the princess, daughter of Demang Lebar Daun. And when night had fallen, the king slept with the princess: and when day dawned he saw that she was not stricken with chloasma. And the king was overjoyed and ordered Demang Lebar Daun to be informed. And Dĕmang Lebar Daun came forthwith, and he too was overjoyed to see that his daughter was unscathed and that no harm had befallen her.

Dĕmang Lebar Daun then made preparations for the ceremonial lustration of Sri Tri Buana, and he ordered a seven-tiered bathing pavilion to be built with five spires. The construction was of the finest quality and it was Bath's workmanship. When it was finished, Dĕmang Lebar Daun initiated the festivities that were to be celebrated day and night for forty days and forty nights, with feasting, drinking and entertainment of every kind, in which participated princes, ministers, courtiers, heralds, war-chiefs and all the people, to the accompaniment of music that rolled like thunder. Many were the buffaloes, oxen and sheep that were slaughtered: the rice-refuse from the cooking-pots was piled mountain-high and the boiling water was like a sea in which the heads of slaughtered buffaloes and oxen were so many islands.

When the forty days and forty nights were accomplished, the ceremonial water was borne in procession to the accompaniment of every sort of music, and the vessels containing the water were all of them of gold studded with jewels. Then Sri Tri Buana with his bride, Princess Wan Sendari, were borne in procession seven times round the pavilion, and they were then lustrated on the central platform, the ceremony being performed by Bath.

After Sri Tri Buana had been living for some time at Palembang he planned to visit the coast and he sent for Děmang Lebar Daun, who came forthwith. And Sri Tri Buana said to him, "I am thinking of going to the coast to find a suitable site for a city. What say you?" And Děmang Lebar Daun replied, "As your Highness pleases. If your Majesty goes, I will accompany you, for I must not be parted from your Highness." Then said Sri Tri Buana, "Please then have ships made ready." And Děmang Lebar Daun did obeisance and left the palace to call men to prepare the craft. When this was done, Děmang Lebar Daun arranged for his younger brother to remain at Palembang in his absence, saying, "I am leaving you here in charge of the city as I am going with his Majesty, accompanying him whenever he may go." And his brother replied, "Very well: no wish of yours will I disobey."

Sri Tri Buana then set forth, he in the royal (golden) yacht for the menfolk and the queen in the silver yacht, while Demang Lebar Daun, the ministers and the war-chiefs had each their own craft. So vast was the fleet that there seemed to be no counting it; the masts of the ships were like a forest of trees, their pennons and streamers were like driving clouds and the state umbrellas of the Rajas like cirrus. So many were the craft that accompanied Sri Tri Buana that the sea seemed to be nothing but ships.

After leaving Kuala Palembang they crossed over the Sělat Sěpat, and from there they sailed on to Sělat Sambar. Meanwhile the news had come to Bentan after they had sailed from Palembang, that "a Raja from Bukit Si-Guntang, who is descended from Raja Iskandar Dzu'l-Karnain, is on his way here and is now at Sělat Sambar."

Now Bentan was ruled by a woman, called Wan Sri Benian, though according to one tradition her name was Queen Sakidar Shah. She was a great Raja, and at that time it was she who visited Sham. It was Queen Sakidar Shah who first instituted the drum of sovereignty, which practice was followed by other Rajas. When she heard the news of the coming of Sri Tri Buana, she commanded her ministers, Indra Bopal and Aria Bopal to bring him to Bentan. [At that time the fleet of Bentan was four hundred sail.] And Wan Sri Benian said to Indra Bopal, "If this Raja is old, say to him 'Your younger sister sends her obeisance', but if he is young, say 'Your mother sends her greetings'."

So Indra Bopal and Aria Bopal set out, and the ships of the party sent to bring Sri Tri Buana to Bentan were strung out in one unbroken line from Tanjong Rungas to Selat Sambar. And when they came up with Sri Tri Buana, Indra Bopal and Aria Bopal perceived that he was very young, and they said to him, "Your mother sends greetings and invites your Highness to Bentan." So Sri Tri Buana proceeded to Bentan and went into the palace to Wan Sri Benian as she was called. Now the purpose of Wan Sri Benian had been to marry Sri Tri Buana, but when she saw how young he was she adopted him instead as her son and shewed such affection for him that she had him installed at Bentan as her successor, to the beat of the drum of sovereignty. After he had been there for a time, Sri Tri Buana one day sought permission to make an expedition to Tanjong Běmian for sport, and the queen replied, "Why go so far afield for your sport, my son? In Bentan are there not deer and mouse-deer with enclosures into which to drive them? Are there not barking-deer and porcupines with cages in which to capture them? Are there not fish in our pools and every sort of fruit and flower in our gardens? Why is it that you want to go so far afield for your sport?" And Sri Tri Buana answered, "If I am not permitted to go, then I shall die, whether I sit down or stand up or whatever I do." Whereupon Wan Sri Benian said, "Rather than you should die, go, my son."

And the queen ordered Indra Bopal and Aria Bopal to have craft made ready. And when that was done, Sri Tri Buana set out with his consort. And the whole fleet — royal yachts, ships for sleeping, ships for the menfolk, wherries that were paddled, kitchen boats, dug-outs for fishing with the casting-net and floating bath-houses — (put out to sea), with a countless host of escorting vessels.

And when they were come to Tanjong Bemian, the king went ashore for a picnic on the sand, and his consort accompanied by the wives of the chiefs went ashore also to picnic on the sand and enjoy herself collecting shellfish. And she sat under a screw-pine, with the wives of the chiefs in attendance upon her, happily watching her handmaids amusing themselves, each one in her own way, some gathering shellfish, some digging up *barai*, some picking mangrove flowers and making nosegays, some picking *teruntum* to wear in their hair, some picking bananas and cooking them, some picking *butun* leaves, some picking sponges and playing with them, some getting sea-worms and making salad with them, some getting seaweed for jelly and salad — all of them disporting themselves to their heart's content, each in her own fashion.

Now Sri Tri Buana and all the men went hunting and great was the quantity of game that fell to them. And it happened that a deer passed in front of Sri Tri Buana and though he speared it in the back, the deer escaped. Sri Tri Buana followed it up and again speared it, this time through the ribs: and the deer could not escape and fell dead. And Sri Tri Buana came to a very large, high rock. He climbed on to the top of this rock and looking across the water he saw that the land on the other side had sand so white that it looked like a sheet of cloth. And he asked Indra Bopal, "What is that stretch of sand that we see yonder? What land is that?" And Indra Bopal answered, "That, your Highness, is the land called Temasek." And Sri Tri Buana said, "Let us go thither." And Indra Bopal replied, "I will do whatever your Highness commands." So Sri Tri Buana embarked and started on the crossing. And when they came out into the open sea, a storm arose and the ship began to fill with water. Bale as they might they could not clear her and the boatswain gave order to lighten the ship. But though much was thrown overboard, they still could not bale the ship dry. She was by now close to Telok Blanga, and the boatswain said to Sri Tri Buana, "It seems to me, your Highness, that it is because of the crown of kingship that the ship is foundering. All else has been thrown overboard, and if we do not do likewise with this crown we shall be helpless with the ship." And Sri Tri Buana replied, "Overboard with it then!" And the crown was thrown overboard. Thereupon the storm abated, and the ship regained her buoyancy and was rowed to land. And when they reached the shore, the ship was brought close in and Sri Tri Buana went ashore with all the ship's company and they amused themselves with collecting shellfish. The king then went inland for sport on the open ground at Kuala Temasek.

And they all beheld a strange animal. It seemed to move with great speed; it had a red body and a black head; its breast was white; it was strong and active in build, and in size was rather bigger than a he-goat. When it saw the party, it moved away and then disappeared. And Sri Tri Buana inquired of all those who were with him, "What beast is that?" But no one knew. Then said Děmang Lebar Daun, "Your Highness, I have heard it said that in ancient times it was a lion that had that appearance. I think that what we saw must have been a lion." And Sri Tri Buana said to Indra Bopal, "Go back to Bentan and tell the queen that now we shall not be returning, but that if she wishes to shew her affection for us, will she furnish us with men, elephants and horses, as we propose to establish a city here at Temasek." And Indra Bopal set forth to return to Bentan: and when he arrived there, he presented himself before Wan Sri Benian to whom he related what Sri Tri Buana had said. "Very well," said Wan Sri Benian, "we will never oppose any wish of our son." And she sent men, elephants and horses without number. Sri Tri Buana then established a city at Temasek, giving it the name of Singapura. And Singapura became a great city, to which foreigners resorted in great numbers so that the fame of the city and its greatness spread throughout the world.

from The Malay Annals, *Oxford University Press.*

Baba Super Superstitions
by Cheo Kim Ban

THE Chinese have their superstitions and Indians have theirs also. The Malays too are not short of taboos but the prize for the most number of *pantangs* must go to the Babas*. They subscribe to everybody's superstitious beliefs.

Most Babas who follow superstitious practices are not even aware that they do, much less know the origins of these beliefs. They practise them lightheartedly and perhaps sheepishly in the same way as those who touch wood or throw spilt salt over their shoulder.

The serious follower is likely to be a Baba over forty and brought up steeped in the belief of spirits, ghosts, shrines and occult practices. His day is a minefield of potential disaster avoided by religious prescriptions or adverted by appropriate remedial actions.

Like all good Babas, his morning begins with a bath and prayers. His first duty is to the gods of heaven and his ancestral spirits. The motive: to invoke their blessing upon himself and his household. He does this with joss-sticks; first at the gate of his house, then before the altar of the kitchen god and finally to his ancestral tablets. Each time, he raises three joss-sticks above his head and asks for a safe and good day.

While the man of the house performs this daily ritual, the women take pain in their dressing. It is especially important that they appear before elders with neatly combed hair, not only for tidiness sake but also because bedraggled hair is a sign of unhappiness and mourning. Similarly, everyone puts on a happy face as they greet each other in turn according to seniority. To start with a sour face, they say, spoils the harmony of the day.

It is breakfast time and no bickering is allowed. Neither can one prop one's chin with one's

---

* *The Babas are a community of people with a unique culture which evolved in Singapore, Malacca and Penang.*

hand. It is a harbinger of bad news. Do it and you will be thrown the caustic remark, "*Kenapa, kapal sudah tenggelam?*", "Why? Has your ship sunk?" — alluding to the days when rich Babas had many ships plying the region. Of course you must be happy, but don't sing at the table. You'll only land yourself an older spouse. Neither should you rush your meal; gobbling implies that your family has not provided you with food regularly. But not too slowly, please — you're eating like the old and sick.

It is forbidden for anyone to be called from the table once a meal has begun, no matter how important the caller may be. Answer the phone between courses and you *patah suap* — break both the rhythm of the meal and of the day. Old folk used to say, "When a person eats, he is a king and should not be disturbed."

On the same principle, never call someone back once he has left the house or even as he leaves the front door. This is *patah langkah* and whatever he sets out to do that day will be left unfinished. Woe betide anyone who asks for money

158

from someone ready to leave home. There are some who take all this so seriously that, once their rhythm is broken, they will refuse to leave the house the whole day.

If you manage to get out safely, watch out for the omens of the world. Be careful if a woman with long hair should come near you. If her hair blows against your face, it is very *sway* — unadulterated bad luck. Some fierce elderly Nonyas have been known to pull the tresses, scold the owner and threaten to cut it off there and then. If they were on their way to play *cherki* (a card game), pity the poor girl...

The razor of life is double-edged. Things were equally bad if you were a monk and met a Nonya on her way to gamble. To her a shaven head can only mean that she would be shorn of her money. So some remedial measure must be taken:

Take a sprig of pomegranate leaf and soak in a bowl of water. Wash hands thoroughly with treated water to get rid of the bad luck.

If ill-luck persists, a more drastic and potent cure is recommended.

Collect water from seven wells and bathe in it. Alternatively, obtain a pot-pourri from the temple, sprinkle liberally in bath water and soak (yourself) till misfortune disappears.

This is *buang sial* — to be rid of bad fortune.

Nonyas, as Baba ladies are called, beside being fastidious are adept at kitchen craft. They have cooked up a whole set of beliefs about cooking called *pertuas*.

Here is a tasting portion.

Pound chillies in even numbers if you don't want them to be too hot. Stop the smarting of chilli in your eyes by eating salt at once. Drink the water from a young coconut to bring down a fever. Always satisfy the craving of a pregnant woman or the baby will drool.

The Nonyas are even careful about the way they look in the kitchen. They warn unmarried girls not to get their sarongs wet because a soaked sarong brought a "soaked" husband — a drunk one. Also, don't forget to smooth down your sarong after working; an upturned hem indicates a green-eyed monster. These, no doubt, were devised to put a check on the carelessness of young girls.

It is more difficult however, to detect the logic of other taboos directed at eligible girls. Figure this one out. An unmarried girl should not drink too much soup or it will rain heavily on her wedding day.

If you should arrive at a home while the family is having a meal, *jumpa jerki*! You meet with good luck! But if you should leave before their meal is over, have the courtesy of going to the nearest diner and touch his plate, saying, "*Ini gantikan*" — "This is a replacement." By touching the plate, you are replacing the luck which you may be taking away from the family's rice bucket when you leave.

Everyone must hurry home before dark. *Senjakala*, the moments between day and night when light fails is considered the most dangerous hour. This is when spirits begin to prowl and when one's own spirit is most vulnerable. No one should sleep while the sun sets. In sleep, part of your being leaves your body making it even more open to evil influences.

The man of the house takes another bath as soon as he gets home and repeats his morning rituals to seek protection for the night. The lights of the house must be switched on. Light dispels evil and to leave the house in darkness is to court trouble.

It is forbidden to sweep or dust the house once the lights come on.

I was told of a lady who liked to sweep her house in the evenings to save time the next day. Her Nonya neighbour warned her several times against this but the advice was not taken. Soon afterwards, the stubborn lady's house was burgled and her husband stabbed to death.

This, by the way, is a true story.

The after-glow of dusk is the colour of the '*mambang kuning*', the 'yellow spirit' which afflict children with jaundice. No mother will take her baby out during this time and pregnant women will stay indoors.

This region of change in time or space: twilight time, the edge of the jungle, the close of a week, the shifting sea and the unreachable horizon, is fraught with peril.

It is dangerous to cut one's nails at twilight; should you cut yourself, the bleeding will not stop. To chew sugar-cane at sunset is to chew on the bones of one's parents. Whistle and you whistle for devils.

An old saw goes, "Mention a person at night and he will come; mention a ghost and it will appear."

Two terrible ghosts are the *pontianak* and *penanggalan*: birth demons. There are two more who worry Babas less. They are *bajang* and *hantu tetek*. The former takes the form of a *musang* or polecat and are said to cause mild fevers and convulsions in children. They also breed quarrels among men. The latter are ghosts with pendulous breasts and if you happen to be caught by one of them, she puts you between her breasts and smothers you to death.

The *penanggalan* swoops about in a phosphorescent glow; only a head and entrails trailing. They avoid objects into which their entrails can be caught. This is why new mothers put thorny screwpine leaves under their beds.

An iron nail is the thing most feared by the *pontianak*. This story reveals why.

A man once ensnared a *pontianak* by driving an iron nail in her head, whereupon she changed into a beautiful maiden. He married her and they had a child. One day, on the pretext that she had lice on her head, she asked the child to pick through her hair. Then the child felt the nail and asked what it was. This was exactly what the demon had been waiting for. She asked the child to pull it out. He did, and the banshee flew screeching away.

Pontianak is the she-demon that

lures men to their doom.

I have been the object of a story about the *pontianak*.

This was during the years I lectured in the English department of the Teachers' Training College in Sabah. I was the only Asian staff there.

A Sandakan Chinese daily ran a story.

It said that a Singaporean Chinese lecturer in English at the Teacher's Training College was driving home late one night from the capital and was flagged down by a beautiful girl near the sixth milestone Chinese cemetery. The teacher apparently gave the girl a ride and when she alighted, the woman gave him some money. At that moment, the beauty was transformed into a hideous hag with fangs and dishevelled hair. The money the teacher held turned into joss paper. He had met a *pontianak*. The story went on to report that the man became very ill but was fortunately found and sent to hospital.

The article could not have been about anyone but myself. I was the only Chinese lecturer from Singapore in the college and was the only one who drove regularly to Jesselton.

The next time I went down-town, I was mobbed by friends and acquaintances. They wanted to know when I had been discharged and asked if I was alright. Meanwhile, my former parish priest who had been transferred up north to Kudat called the College to ask if it was true I had died of shock.

It was all a mystery to me, especially when they mentioned *pontianak*. When I denied it, everyone thought I had lost my mind after all.

The story was, of course, a fabrication but many years later when I dropped in at an old haunt when I was on business in Sabah, the Baba bartender rushed forward and shook my hand. He remembered the story and was amazed that I was still alive!

It is a wonder that a superstitious Baba can have a peaceful night's sleep with all these ghosts flitting through his subconscious.

It was not just ghosts though, that bothered the Babas.

If a moth flew into his room at night, it was quickly told: "If you bring good news, stay; otherwise, fly away." And any grasshopper or praying mantis that strayed into a Baba house after dark had its head twisted off. If you see someone doing such a thing, do not think that he is being cruel; killing insects for pleasure. He is only protecting himself. Should the insect have a grain of rice in its neck, it was a *polong* or *pelesit* — a familiar spirit kept by an enemy who had sent it to his house to do him harm.

Baba households had failsafe precautions to protect the house and members of the family.

Paper charms obtained from temples are pasted over the lintel of the main door. If not, a mirror to deflect evil, a *pak kua* (or trigram) to confuse demons and a piece of netting to capture spirits attempting to enter the house is put in its stead. In addition, a copy of *The Book of Fate* could be hung behind the same door, alternatively a broom placed upside down at the same place is said to be equally effective. You could add a twig of the *kelor* or 'drumstick' tree to the collection of paraphernalia already hanging

over the lintel, but to have special protection against robbers who use black magic to put the entire household into a deep sleep, rear a climbing perch. A quick precaution is to place a small stone mortar inside the Shanghai jar of drinking water. However, no solution could be more convenient or simple than leaving the evening's rice-pot unwashed and filled with water overnight. Don't forget to put the ladle in the pot to make it effective.

There is one last thing to look after.

Make sure that the foot of your bed does not face an entrance. That is the way coffins are positioned; a corpse is always placed with its feet pointing towards the door. The principle is that a person comes into the world head first and departs, head last.

Having taken every precaution, the Baba and Nonya can now sleep soundly.

Perhaps not. There is the realm of dreams to contend with.

Dreaming of a tooth falling out means that a relative will die; if the gum bleeds, the relative is a close one. But if you dream of someone dying, that person will have long life. It is not a comforting thing to have a dead friend or relative appear in your dream, especially if he invites you to stay with him or go on a long journey. Strangely, dreaming of excreta is a sign of a coming windfall.

Then there are the gamblers who are desperate enough to sleep on a grave, hoping to dream of lucky numbers. Better still if they see themselves on the pot writing the numbers. Jackpot!

Sleepwalkers should not be awakened suddenly, the fright is bad for his soul. But slap someone who gnashes his teeth in his sleep; he is gnashing away his parents' lives.

Finally, don't paint a sleeping person's face or even comb his hair. His soul wanders to far-away places in slumber and when he returns to find an altered face, he does not recognize it as his own, is stressed, and causes the cord connecting body and spirit to snap. He will die.

By now, you must imagine Babas as neurotic, quaking beings, nervous at the slightest provocation. Let me categorically state that this is not true. I am a Baba and we modern Babas have discarded our superstitions. I give you my word on it, or I'll meet a *pontianak* tonight.

Chinese gentlemen, circa 1900.

Two Pioneers Remember
by Yvonne Quahe

KWEK Hong Png and Ho Yeow Koon were two poor boys from the Province of Fukien. Like those who came before them to Nanyang, they had dreams of becoming wealthy and successful.

In the early 1900s, it was common knowledge that Singapore and Malaya were the lands of promise. There was work available here: jobs in the tin mines or on rubber plantations, opportunities to be contract labourers or perhaps an assistant to a merchant. At least it provided the assurance of the next meal and for the more hopeful, the chance of making a mint. It was this prospect that led droves of Chinese from Southern China to leave their homeland and head for Peninsula Malaya. For decades this was true.

Kwek and Ho had come to Singapore eleven years apart, 1928 and 1939 respectively, but their reasons for leaving their homes were similar. Life in China was exceedingly difficult. Chaos, poverty and weak government had taken its toll.

Day in and day out, Kwek and his family toiled in the fields. They survived hand to mouth. There had to be a better way, a better place.

'Life was difficult, so one day my father said to me: "Why don't you leave and go to the Nanyang to make a living."'

So Kwek Hong Png went.

'I had to take some vehicular transport and then a boat before I could get from Tong An to Amoy. At Amoy I had to wait for two to three days for a boat to leave for the Nanyang. I was of such a slight build that I managed to get my ticket for half-price ($8).

'That was for a common berth and that meant passengers rolled out a mat, used a blanket and that is how it was. There were three meals a day. During meal time, you had to go to the galley and ask for rice and vegetables.

'The boat was called *Talma Apcar*; you could say it was an *ang-moh* (foreign) boat. It was quite dirty and many were sick on board. The voyage to Singapore took ten days.'

No matter how lean their harvest, at least the Kweks had one to boast of. Ho Yeow Koon and his family lived in a village surrounded by rocky mountains and precious little could be grown on that barren land.

'My home village was very poor. At the back of the village was a rocky mountain with no soil cover, so our family was indeed poor. You couldn't plant anything so, our staple diet was melons; if it wasn't melon gruel, it was melon soup. Occasionally we would add a few peanuts. We also had "flowery porridge" — this was because there was not enough rice so that they appeared like flowers floating in the melon gruel... At that time, we had to wait for I don't know how many months before we could have a meal of rice.'

Ho's ancestors were wealthy. The only remnant of their wealth was the ancestral home shared by several kinsmen. His father never got accustomed to having to work so it was left up to his mother to fend for the family.

'My family were the poorest of families in the village. My father belonged to the "fallen" generation of the family, he not only did not have a livelihood but also could not find work to make a living. My mother, besides selling two children, had another four young children. She had bound feet and so she could not farm. My father did not know what hard work and labour was so my mother often — and this I noticed myself and was also told by her — for the sake of making a living would use her skills at handicraft to tailor some clothes, weave and make some children's shoes, stomach warming girdles and aprons for sale.

'My mother would have two meals while we had three. Sometimes, my two sisters would also, like my mother, have two meals while we ate three. This was when males were held in higher regard than females. The saying was that men were more important so allow him to eat his fill.

'Besides these troubles, there was, in the feudal society of the village,

Chinese farmer with bullock cart team, circa 1910.

the practice of laughing at the poor and revering the rich. So although the poor could barely live, they also had to bear being looked down upon.'

Ho Yeow Koon's father had come to Nanyang himself to redeem a fortune, but after thirteen long years he returned, still poor, to die twenty-four days after his homecoming. Ho's mother then went with the children to her family.

It was at that time that Ho Yeow Koon, aged fifteen, started work in a transport brigade doing odd jobs.

This meant long hours of work regardless of weather conditions. His wages didn't even amount to two dollars a month but at least food was provided. 'So long as each of us had food it was already good enough.'

This cruel childhood, seeing his mother toil from dusk till dawn to scratch a living ignited in him a desire to study and work hard. One day he would show her his gratitude.

The more Ho thought about it, the clearer it became that Nanyang was his only hope, the key to his aspirations. It had been suggested that his uncle who was there be his patron but help was not forthcoming.

Addresses of relatives and letters of recommendation were great prizes to those who hoped to leave China. For many, these meant a roof over their head or an opportunity for employment when they reached their destination. It amounted to a sponsorship and because of the heavy responsibility it added to those already in Nanyang, people with relatives there kept addresses a well guarded secret and were judicious in issuing letters of introduction.

'Addresses of relatives in Nanyang was not something you gave people carelessly.'

One could go alone but it meant being registered as a common coolie, resigned to virtual slavery. Those who went that way were called 'pigs'.

In the end, it was only the perseverance of Ho's mother that brought the long awaited address. She had plied this uncle's family with gifts and wrote every week pleading with him to send money for the passage.

Ho now had an address but still no money. At that point, a crisis surfaced in his life. A decision had to be made. The Sino-Japanese War had begun and the Red Army was swelling its ranks.

'When I was seventeen or eighteen, there was a draft. It was the turning point of my life. The brother of my old employer was a commander and he asked me to become a soldier. But my mother still hoped I could get to Nanyang; so with the help of my employer and some colleagues, I finally got an immigration pass. You could say that my boss's brother helped because it was not easy to escape (the draft) and he allowed me to go.'

Ho got out of China to Hongkong; that first vital step to Nanyang had been taken. There was still no passage money but at least he was on his way.

In Hongkong, he waited and worked as a cook by day and cared for his employer's child by night, rocking the baby to sleep in his arms. His own bed was a double deckered platform tucked under a staircase.

After a total of four years' begging and hoping, the money for the voyage finally arrived.

'A distant uncle in Hongkong bought the ticket for me and contacted the sailors of the ship too. In the past, if you had the money you would stay in a cabin but those without the means would be put in the cargo hold. I still had a little money which my mother gave me so he arranged a sailor's berth for me to sleep in.'

To Ho, this was an unnecessary luxury, but there was a reason for the extravagance.

'Compared to the sleeping accommodation under the staircase, it really didn't matter (that he got a berth). But they hoped that if I bunked with the sailors, I would not need to go through quarantine and suffer during those two or three days.

'This was why my uncle arranged it all. He also gave me five dollars and another twenty cents which was for the rickshaw fare from Tanjong Pagar to Upper Circular Road.'

So finally in September 1939 Ho Yeow Koon set sail for Singapore.

Would all this be worth it — the restless waiting, the uneasy nights, the humiliation of his mother's begging? Was Singapore a golden horizon or an empty dream?

'The ship berthed at Wharf No. 4 at Tanjong Pagar. We queued up for immigration but because I had a sailor's bunk, the health formalities were simpler. We paid five dollars and supplied a photograph of ourselves (this was prepared in Hongkong). This is how I came, just a bundle of a few clothes and nothing else.'

Ho Yeow Koon had finally arrived at his destination but his future was far from assured. Knotted with fear and trepidation, the young man made his way to his uncle's house.

The new sights and sounds, the soaking heat, the babble of alien tongues made no impression. His whole being was wrapped in anxious anticipation of his uncle's welcome.

'The first thing was to get my uncle to take me in... I was immature and it was my first time in Nanyang so the main aim was to find a job and earn a few dollars to send home to my mother.'

The gods must have smiled down benevolently at Ho.

'I must thank my uncle. He immediately said that I could stay there

Cosmopoltan crowd in Fullerton Square just beyond Johnston's pier, circa 1910.

— although it had much to do with the letter from his mother (to whom he was very dutiful). I should remember that he gave me one or two dollars but I am not very sure... Yes, I should remember that he gave me a dollar or two and at least wrote a letter to my mother on my behalf to say that I had arrived.'

Deeply relieved and grateful, Ho settled into his new life. Home was a shophouse in Chinatown.

'This building had two and a half floors and the top floor was occupied by someone from our village. My uncle and his wife slept on the second floor. I slept downstairs on my uncle's table.'

Unlike Ho Yeow Koon who could afford a sailor's berth, Kwek Hong Png came out as a deck passenger and suffered the fate of being quarantined.

'When we were near Singapore, we were not allowed to go ashore and we all had to go to St John's Island to get innoculated. This was for a week. There were two or three of those from the boat who cut open kerosene tins. Then we were rationed some rice. We washed and cooked it in the tins. We were also given sardines, a bit of preserved soya beans and salted vegetables.'

Kwek was in sight of the golden shore but could not go to it. Days passed slowly.

The day finally arrived when they were taken by lighters to Johnston's Pier.

It was four or five in the afternoon. Kwek hailed a rickshaw to take him to his uncle's house. Would he be ignored, humiliated, turned away?

'"I have never seen you before. You are still so young; why have you come to Nanyang!" My uncle saw that I was still a child.

'I said, "My father in China has a hard life and he said to come to Nanyang to see if I could find the opportunity to become an apprentice, to study at night if possible.

'My relative became silent and did not say anything else for sometime.

'Finally, he said, "It is a good idea. Why don't I bring you to my house and you can stay there temporarily." I stayed there for seven or eight months.'

For both Kwek and Ho, the first hurdle had been crossed. Their relatives had not turned them away. They were determined to make good in their new world.

'So long as you could get to your destination, you would cross mountains of swords and mountains of fire and be prepared to endure hardship. You thought of nothing else.'

These youths of seventeen and nineteen were already well-schooled in endurance. Jobs for the Sin Kheh (new immigrant) were not easy to come by even with the help of relatives.

Kwek used to ask his uncle every day:

'Sir, you must find a shop where I can *tumpang* (board) so that I can become an apprentice. I will not want a salary.

'At that time, the economic climate made it difficult to find jobs, not to say one where I could board.'

Kwek's first job was that of a shop assistant. The working day started at 4 a.m.; by 6 a.m. the floors had to be swept and the tables cleaned. The first customers would arrive between six and seven. Sometimes, he had to work overtime and there wasn't even a moment to stop for a meal. However, he was obstinate in his determination to succeed.

'When the boss gave me definite duties, I did them. That is to say I had the ability and did not shy away from difficult tasks. I had the ability to learn, to do work. I did whatever work there was to do. My salary was at the most $5 to $6. Very cheap. Of this $5 to $6, about $2 was sent back to China. $1 was for night school and I would try to save a little.

'All I knew was that I was very interested in the line of work. Each of us must not be afraid of difficulties. If we want to learn something we peg away at it until we succeed. That is why we must do it even if it is difficult. If you fear difficulties, then it will be hard for you to succeed.'

He had dreams of starting his own business.

'One day, when opportunity knocks, and I have the capital, I will be my own boss. At that time my dreams and hopes will be achieved. This was what I believed.'

This was what fuelled his impetus. Ho learned by careful observation, he tackled adversity and saved all he could towards his goal.

Such perseverance, initiative and dedication did not go unnoticed. Kwek Hong Png's employer saw it all and promotion was inevitable.

Ho Yeow Koon also started life as an assistant in a rice merchant's shop.

'I did odd jobs around the place. Initially, I had to clean the place from the ground floor to the top. I had a colleague, Lim Chiaw Bak: we shared the work. We also had to wash the toilet buckets everyday. It was changed once a day and we had to wash them everytime it was changed. We had to spring clean once a week.

'My employer had a rule. We could only keep one forty watt lamp on in the whole three floors. If there were two lights on he'd have something to say.'

Thrift and debt, long hours of work, poor living conditions, meagre salaries and exacting bosses were hallmarks of a Sin Kheh's existence.

'I arrived in April and did not receive any salary till December. But I got $12 for meals and forty cents for haircuts.

'Of the $12, I had a balance of $5 to send to my mother. I washed my own clothes, both day clothes and underwear. My boss had two haircuts a month. I had one so that I could save twenty cents. So I knew I had to stay about the shop 365 days a year and not go out.'

In fact Ho Yeow Koon had the rare privilege of a choice of two jobs.

'One opportunity was this job which was like working in a colonial firm. This was an eight to six job so I could study at night, write letters, learn to use the abacus or go out and look around. The other job was with my god-brother who asked me to go to the Almond Village Restaurant to be an apprentice. This is equivalent to today's "boy", that is, we had to serve food and wash dishes. The salary was better but I did think that I should stay where I was because I did get $12 of which I

Chinese barber and earcleaner.

could send $5 to my mother to support her. At least she could then have two out of three meals a day. And she certainly could find some way of getting another meal. So I stuck to the job and I received a salary of $6 a month (in addition to expenses) the next year.'

He was shadowed by his ambition to show her his gratitude.

Ho soon realized that in order to succeed in any measure, he would have to be 'nurtured' by his boss. It was crucial that he gained favour by diligence.

'My boss had some accounts which he wanted me to copy. He said that I had to do it that night as he could not wait till the next day. He lived at the Old Market next to the Chiau Siang Club. He had another home opposite the Chinese Chamber of Commerce.

'He would go to his club to play cards and games and come to the shop at eleven or twelve at night and asked me to copy some things to be handed up the next morning. He knew that I could do it because I was willing to learn.'

SINGAPORE SLING

It was a hard fact of Sin Kheh life that many employers demanded more than their rightful pound of flesh. The Sin Kheh was at his beck and call; every waking hour belonged to the boss.

Most shop assistants or apprentices lived in the business premises. There was a great sense of camaradrie especially when it came to a mean, stingy boss.

'As my employer dealt in rice, we made use of it and cooked our own meals every morning and night. We went to the Hokkien market street and bought food to go with the rice. This would cost twenty to thirty cents a time. We did not have to pay for the rice. We just used it, used it without permission. We also secretly used the boss's stove to cook. He would come in at eight in the morning but we would wake up at six o'clock to cook the porridge so that by the time he arrived the stove would already be cold. If it was still hot, he would surely have a few words for us. So we had to steal before six-thirty in the morning. We only cooked on the stove at night after he went off. We had our mid-day meal in a coffee shop in Market Street.'

But sadly, in the end, it was the bosses who had the last word.

The Sin Kheh's future hung in the balance of their grasp.

Not long after he arrived, Ho Yeow Koon experienced this real threat.

'This was in 1940, the economy was not good and the Japanese were heading southwards. At that time, the company I worked for was to retrench three people so I slogged my life away so I would not be retrenched. It was no problem if I had no meals but how can my mother go without her meals? So I persevered.

'One night, when... (my employer) was about to go home, he could not hail a rickshaw and I had to run to the Central Police Station to get the rickshaw for him. When he saw me all sweaty and ready to expire, he said: "Why are you so silly. Why didn't you sit in the rickshaw and get him to pull you back here? You followed him on foot, you silly fellow!" So he scolded me and I explained that I did not dare do that. He then said: "I know you looked worried the whole day long but don't worry, you will not be the one to be retrenched." That night I slept very soundly.'

Perhaps in this deep sleep he dreamt of a prosperous business group called Keck Seng. They dealt initially in local produce like pigs and duck eggs. Then this small business grew and diversified. There was now a hotel by the river, near his godowns. They were all his. At last he was able to show his mother his gratitude.

When he awoke he had to nudge himself to reality. At least he had a job.

Today, the two boys are no longer poor. They head large business conglomerates. Kwek Hong Png's Hong Leong and Ho Yeow Koon's Keck Seng have interests spanning finance, real estate, manufacturing and construction.

These pioneers had worked their dreams into reality.

Yvonne Quahe is the author of We Remember: Cameos of Pioneer Life, *Landmark Books, 1986.*

Distinguished Chinese gentleman.

KIMMY
by Ovidia Yu

FRANKIE Ong was one of the junior counsellors at the YMCA camp that year. Junior Counsellors did all the things that counsellors couldn't be bothered with — like counting kids before swimming, counting kids after swimming, keeping kids quiet during rest hours, and rummaging in the storeroom for extra bedding.

Another of their duties was waiting, after the camp was over, for the last kids to be picked up by their parents. Which was why Frankie Ong was waiting with Kitty and me in the nearly closed up hall at 7 p.m., with all the fans off and all the chairs folded up and stacked against the walls.

Frankie Ong was looking terribly irritated. All the other kids had left by 5 p.m. and all the other counsellors had gone too. I kept very quiet. It's better to be quiet when people are in a Mood. Mom was very often in a Mood. Right at that moment, however, she was in Indonesia with Uncle Wang, so it wasn't any good Frankie Ong calling our apartment every ten minutes like he was doing. Mom had sacked Ah Lan and Geok Mui like she did every now and then, and there was no one about to answer the phone.

I told Frankie that Mom wouldn't be back in Singapore for another week, at least, but Kitty said, "Don't listen to Kimmy, she's an awful liar."

Since Kitty was twelve and two years older than me, Frankie Ong believed her. I didn't mind. I wouldn't tell him that Mom had said for the fortune she forked out for the camp and everything they could damnwell keep us a week more. He probably wouldn't have believed that either.

Frankie strode over to the telephone. (Again).

"I'm hungry," I whined to Kitty, because I was.

"Oh, shut up," Kitty said impatiently. She was trying to hear what

Frankie Ong was saying over the phone, but she dug into her bag and gave me a stick of Wrigley's Juicy Fruit gum. I put it into my mouth, but it didn't help much. I decided to listen to Frankie too. He was just saying ...

" — just the two of them. Kitty and Kimmy Seow. Twelve and nine — "

"I'm ten," I said, but he didn't listen. Nobody listens to me, but that doesn't bother me.

" — no, they aren't crying or anything. No, not upset at all ... I've been trying but no one answers ... but it's already seven-something, I can't stay here all night ..."

Then he made a lot of listening noises like "Yeah, I see" "Uh-huh" and finally, "OK — OK — OK" in a frustrated sort of tone. Then he came back to us.

"You're sure there's no one else I can call to come and pick you up?"

"You could call our grandparents" I said, "except —"

"Except what?" Frankie Ong demanded.

"Except they live in Hong Kong." Kitty snapped, "Stop that Kimmy!"

I was staggering around, pretending I had been shot in the stomach. I staggered a bit more and fell down on the floor. Kitty nudged me with her foot.

"You'll have to excuse her," she said, "Kimmy's very young for her age."

"Which is ten, not nine." I put in.

"The floor's dirty, Kimmy." Frankie Ong hauled me to a sitting position then sat down beside me on the dirty floor.

"Look, you two, suppose I call a taxi and send you back first."

"The apartment's all locked up," I said.

"Always is when Mom's out," Kitty added. "Look, Frankie, why don't you just go on home. Mom will turn up sooner or later and we'll be just fine till she does. I can handle Kimmy till then."

"I don't need to be handled," I said.

"I think you should just go on home first," Kitty said again. I knew what she was planning. She had the key to the backdoor of Mom's Lucky Plaza boutique. We could slip in once it closed and spend the night there.

"I can't just leave you here alone like that." Frankie Ong said wearily. "I just spoke to Mr Tan on the phone. He said to just wait and see what happens."

"I was counting 'justs' on my fingers, having noted that Frankie used them a lot.

"What we could do is go back to my place first. I live quite near here. We can leave a note with the *jaga* with my address and you kids come back with me first. Could your parents have had an accident?"

"It'll be in the papers tomorrow," Kitty shrugged.

"Is there any dinner at your place?" I asked.

"Yes." Frankie Ong said. That seemed to settle things. He went off to find the *jaga*.

"But what if Mom comes here?" I asked Kitty.

"She won't, Dummy," Kitty said.

"But you said wasn't it that she was turning up?"

"Oh, Shut up, Kimmy," Kitty said.

I shut up and followed them out. Kitty carried my bag for me.

What Mr Tan knew about Kathryn Seow was that she owned a modelling agency, two boutiques and shares in a restaurant. She was a very rich lady. Very rich ladies often donated large sums of money to institutions that were nice to their little girls. Very rich ladies were also often absent-minded. No reason at all, Mr Tan told Frankie Ong, to make a fuss or call the police just because she hadn't picked up her daughters after the camp. Frankie Ong would simply have to keep an eye on them for a few days, just until their mother turned up. She would be very apologetic, very grateful.

What Mr Tan didn't know about Kathryn Seow was a great deal more interesting. When, as a teenager, she'd arrived in Singapore (from Hong Kong) she'd had a brief affair with an American businessman.

The American businessman started her off on her modelling career and still sent her money for Kitty and tips on high fashion. (He was in that line too). That was why Kathryn Seow rather liked Kitty, even though Kitty had a square jaw, a flat nose and showed great potential as a wrestler. Once she had broken Kimmy's arm across her knee, rather like one might break a ruler. Kitty had been much nicer to Kimmy after that. Kathryn hadn't really minded. She didn't like Kimmy much.

Kimmy was small and some people said she was pretty. She looked like her father, who had looked a lot like Malcom MacDowell. Kathryn Seow had meant to marry him, but after a few months together in London, (she had been at a designer's course, he studying dentistry) he had gone back to Australia and promptly married a childhood sweetheart. When Kimmy was born (back in Singapore) Kathryn sent her off to him care of Qantas. Ron sent the baby right back, without even a note, but plus a bad cold. Kathryn put the baby in the oven and turned on the gas, but the servant took her out before she suffocated. After that, Kathryn kept Kimmy around, though she sacked the servant. She still didn't like Kimmy very much, though. Kimmy was beginning to look a lot like Malcolm MacDowell.

Mr Tan didn't know all this, so he couldn't have told Frankie Ong, who consequently didn't believe Kimmy when she said that her father was in Australia and Kitty's father in America. Kitty said that Kimmy would never accept it, but their father had been American and had P-A-S-S-E-D A-W-A-Y in '76. Frankie Ong deduced that Kimmy was a sensitive kid with a vivid imagination.

We stayed at Frankie Ong's house for five days altogether. Frankie Ong's father was really dead. They had a picture of him in the living room and they had tins of joss-sticks in front of it. Frankie Ong's mother put a plate of fruit in front of it too. Because she only spoke Malay and Hokkien, we had a hard time communicating. Our servants had only spoken Cantonese and that was all I could speak.

Frankie had three brothers at home — Danny, Bobby and Kenny. There were two sisters too, Mei Lin and Mei Hwa. Another sister was studying in Australia. I told him that that was where my father was, but he didn't believe me.

I really liked it in Frankie Ong's house. It was huge, and on stilts even though it wasn't any place near the sea. I thought it was on stilts so that when the sea came up it wouldn't get wet, but Mrs Ong told me it was for when it flooded during rainstorms. I hoped and hoped that it would rainstorm while we were there so I could see the water come right up the drive and under the house but it didn't rain a drop. I'm not a very lucky person.

Frankie Ong grew resigned to having us there. He still made frantic phone calls to Mr Tan but they were sounding less frantic after Mr Tan had got in touch with Emmelina, the manageress of Mom's boutique in Specialist Centre and Mr Anderson, Mom's lawyer, and been told by both of them that Mom was on a working holiday, she was often absent-minded and to please keep an eye on the girls while they tried to get in touch with her.

Once Frankie knew for sure we wouldn't be stuck with him for good, he became better tempered. In fact, he was pretty nice and Mrs Ong, his mother, was simply wonderful. She was a great cook and never slapped anybody. She asked about the scar that ran down my back from my ear. She saw it when she was plaiting up my hair. I told her that I'd fallen onto a glass coffee table and smashed it and Mom just sliced down my back with a sliver of glass to teach me a lesson for not taking care of her things. Mrs Ong's other son Danny looked and said, "How many stitches?" Danny was studying to be a doctor.

"Oh rubbish," Kitty said when asked. "Kimmy's always making up stories like that. She broke the table and cut herself, that's all. Don't listen to her — she's an awful liar."

Frankie pulled me onto his lap. He often did that after he got to like us better. I liked it too. It felt cosy. I started pulling the pens out of his pocket. He always had coloured felt pens that I liked to draw with.

"Did your mother — no, put that down, Kimmy, and listen to me —

Kimmy, sit still — tell me honestly — did your mother really do that to you?"

I tried to wriggle off his lap, but he wouldn't let me.

"No," I said. Then I giggled and sang in Kitty's voice, "I'm an awful liar!"

"Stop that!" Kitty said, but she wasn't really mad at me. Later on she slipped out and bought me a packet of dried coconut strips from the Indian shop down the road. Kitty was very good to me.

Finally, we heard from Mom herself. She called one night and talked to Frankie and Mrs Ong. She charmed them completely. She's a very charming person and she smells very good too. She said she would arrive in Singapore on Thursday night and come over to pick us up on Friday.

"I don't want to go home," I told Frankie. "Can't you keep me?"

"So sweet, she is," Bobby Ong said. He patted my cheek. I stuck out my tongue at him, rudely.

"Kimmy!" said Frankie sternly, meaning it wasn't right. I wound my arms around him and stuck out my tongue at him too, but not nastily.

"Who wants to keep you? You're so naughty!" Frankie said. He stroked my hair. "Your mother doesn't want you. I don't want you, what is Kimmy going to do? ... No, Kimmy, I was just joking Kimmy, come, don't cry, of course your mother wants you ..."

Mrs Ong put her arms around me and scolded her son for talking about my mother in front of me. Of course I missed my mother, but never mind, tomorrow she would be back and I would be able to go home and everything would be all right.

Mrs Ong let me do the washing up with her, which I liked very much. They washed all their plates and things by hand, one by one, with just a mop thing, and soap water out of an old ice-cream tub.

Frankie taught Kitty and Kimmy to play checkers. He played three games with Kimmy, then it was Kitty's turn. Kitty played to win, biting her lower lip in determination, and he was finding it harder and harder to beat her. Concentrating, they forgot all about Kimmy, who wandered into Frankie and Bobby's room to look at Frankie's old Marvell comics, at the bottom of the cupboard.

Suddenly, Kimmy screamed, and again and again. Kitty was on her feet and away before Frankie knew what was happening. By the time he reached the bedroom, Kitty was on her knees beside the sobbing Kimmy, rocking her gently. Bobby, still wet from his shower, was standing uncomfortably against the wall, holding his towel in front of him.

"I don't know." He said in response to Frankie's queries, "I didn't see her ... I just came in and started dressing — and then she saw me and just screamed and screamed. I didn't do anything — I didn't. I think she hit her head on the shelf. I don't know what happened to her."

Kimmy was clinging to her sister, just clinging to her and crying and trembling. She had wet herself. Frankie had never seen anyone so terrified before. She reminded him of the white rabbit he had once had to chloroform for a biology practical.

"It's all right," Kitty was soothing her. Obviously this was nothing new to her. "No one's going to hurt you. See? I've made him go away, there's no one going to hurt you. Kitty's going to make it all right. Don't cry. It's all right."

Kimmy began to calm down. She cried more naturally, instead of in the harsh sobs that were half screams. Kitty went on rocking her gently, but it was clear that the worst was over.

"What was that?" Frankie asked, very subdued. He wondered if it could have been a fit. He had never seen anyone in a fit, but had heard it was frightening, and what he had just seen was frightening.

"Uncle Wang — he's our Mom's husband — sometimes he hurts Kimmy. She's always like this when — I think she's just a bit scared. She must have thought Bobby — I mean, if she just saw him there without his clothes on, she must have thought —"

Bobby was frightened nearly to tears himself. "I didn't see her," he protested. "I mean, she was sitting on the floor behind your bed, how was I to ..."

Mrs Ong and her daughters had arrived by then, demanding in excited Hokkien to be told exactly what had happened.

Kitty, who had already picked up quite a bit of Hokkien, told them that Kimmy had slipped and knocked her head on the shelf. She showed them the bruise. Kimmy always made a great fuss about nothing, she said. She looked sharply at Frankie and Bobby, who remained silent; Bobby in relief, Frankie in growing bewilderment.

Kitty put Kimmy to bed and stroked her till she went to sleep. Frankie went in to see her later. The bruise was swollen and angry red on her left temple. Danny had offered to put something on it, but his attempts to look at the damage only brought fresh tears from Kimmy. Danny gave up, with dirty looks at Bobby, muttering that no one got hysterics over a little knock on the head.

Frankie asked Kitty what it was that their stepfather had done to Kimmy that frightened her so much. Kitty couldn't remember what she had said — she had been too worried about Kimmy — and didn't know what he was talking about.

In their room, Bobby was still miserably insisting, "I didn't do anything to frighten her, you know. I wouldn't."

"Yeah, yeah." Frankie was vaguely sorry for his brother, but had other things on his mind. It was Kitty that most worried him. What Kitty had told Bobby and himself when her guard was down, what she had fabricated for his mother and sisters. Her denying the original story later. Kitty lied.

Lying in bed, his mind went over and over Kimmy's stories, but Kimmy was a liar. But they only had that on Kitty's word, and Kitty was a liar. He had just seen for himself. What if Kimmy hadn't been lying? Then their mother was a monster. But he had spoken to their mother himself and she had been a sweet, charming woman.

When he finally fell asleep, Frankie dreamt of an enormous woman holding a crying Kimmy between thumb and forefinger and slashing her back with a glass shard. There was blood all over, and the little Kimmy was struggling to get to him, 'I don't want to go home' it whimpered, 'can't you keep me?' Frankie woke in a cold sweat. In the hot, dark room he could hear Bobby muttering in his sleep, 'I didn't, I didn't, I didn't.' Frankie did not dare go back to sleep.

The next day, he asked Kimmy what it was her Uncle Wang had done that scared her so much. A very subdued, red-eyed Kimmy shrugged. She was all dressed up, ready to be picked up by her mother. She scuffed one small foot against the other.

"Oh nothing," she said carelessly. "I guess I lied about that."

"It was Kitty that told me about that. Does Kitty lie too?"

"No. Only me."

"Then tell me what happened."

Kimmy looked confused, "I thought it was a lie. Did it really happen then? But Kitty told me it was a lie. I don't know. It's so hard to tell. Will you play checkers with me? Will you let me win? Just one more time? Please? Please? Before Mom comes, just one more time, please?"

They played checkers and he let her win. Winning made her so happy because Kimmy didn't get to win very often.

It was nice to see Mom again. She had bought a new car and had a new boyfriend with her. When Kitty asked, she said Uncle Wang had had to stay in Indonesia on a business thing. I wasn't sorry.

"Silly little goosey," Mom said, "What have you done to your face?" She touched her fingers lightly on my forehead. It hurt and I pushed her hand away.

"It was because of that horrible man without any clothes on," I started to explain.

"What horrible —" Mom began. Kitty stepped in as usual.

"Oh Mom, you know how Kimmy makes up stories. She was clumsy and knocked her head looking for comics, that's all: Don't listen to her."

"Was it true?" Mom asked me. "Kimmy, tell me the truth now."

I wasn't sure what I was supposed to say. I edged away from Mom. Kitty shook her head sharply and I was relieved.

"No — It was just a lie — I'm sorry — Mom, please don't hit me, —"

The last came out as a half-scream as she raised her hand, but it was only to brush back a wisp of hair. I felt really stupid and giggled nervously.

"Kimmy —" both Mom and Frankie said at the same time. But they both stopped there and did not go on. Just stood there staring at each other with horrible looks on their faces. Kitty shut her eyes like she was praying. I fidgeted. Still they did not move, but it was like they had a lot to say, only it wouldn't come out. I wondered if it was really happening or whether it would turn out to be another lie, but I couldn't ask Kitty. She wasn't moving either, and her eyes were still closed. Mom's new boyfriend cleared his throat. He was dark like a Malay, but had a Chinese face.

"Children have such vivid imaginations, don't they?" he said. "If you'll let us know how much — I mean, we'll give you something for keeping an eye on the girls. They had a good time, I'm sure. When I was young it was quite an adventure ..."

But no one was listening to him. Mom and Frankie could have been stone, but their eyes were alive, and how they hated each other. I thought they could just be standing there forever.

Swinging Sixties Singapore Style
by Siva Choy

STANDING at the junction of Stamford Road and North Bridge Road, I gaze in awe at Raffles City Complex and the tallest hotel in the world.

Seventy storeys!

At the beginning of the sixties, when we were ludicrously short of tall buildings, I remember a hotel that was so proud it was seven stories high it billed itself the 7th Storey Hotel.

But that wasn't our only skyscraper then. There were at least a couple of buildings ten-storeys high (and both were quite well-known since quite a few people used to jump off them. Jumping off tall blocks was just beginning to replace suicide by hanging or swallowing caustic soda.)

But the building that took the cake was the Asia Insurance Building, all 21-storeys of it, It was THE building to be photographed against, except that with a Brownie camera, you would have had to stand near Clifford Pier to get it all in.

The Asia building was a biggie alright. It was on the postcards and it even got into quiz programmes and you had to be either a fool or a disloyal subversive not to know that if you stuck it anywhere in the continental shelf, its head would be above water.

I don't think Mrs Moonlight Sim (that name's for real), our geog teacher, ever thought there'd come a day when our shipyards would be turning out drilling rigs a lot taller than the good old Asia Building. Not to mention Mount Faber (all 113 metres of it).

One thing that the Asia Building doesn't have, if you think about it, is a car park. In the sixties, you didn't really need them since any place in the street which hadn't been taken up by a hawker stall was yours. As for paying for parking .... the only fellow you'd have had to pay would have been the "jaga kreta" the street urchin who for ten or twenty cents (unlimited parking hours) would make sure he didn't scratch your paintwork or make off with your tyres.

And what if you refused to pay him his few cents and came back to find your car had been redecorated or overhauled? You would most probably have cursed your luck and gone home. Any attempt to hunt down the aforesaid urchin for retribution would probably have ended in a street battle with his gangster protectors. For the early sixties were still the heyday of the triads.

Triads?

Okay, how do I begin explaining triads to anybody who wasn't around at that time. Never mind the historical background — it's easiest to describe them as the Singapore equivalent of the warring mafia gangs of Chicago in the thirties. No, the local boys didn't go around in Chevvies armed with machine guns. They mostly travelled in Hillman cars (Hillmans? Never mind again) armed with long knives, bicycle chains, bearing scrapers, pieces of steel pipe and light-bulbs filled with sulphuric acid.

There were a lot of them around and they made a lot of money offering protection to people who didn't need it and couldn't afford it, like hawkers and tradesmen. The protection racket ("20 cents a week will do, since you're all schoolboys") got so competitive that if you were a teenager and didn't feel an affinity for any one gang, you had to be either the son of a cop or a middle-class wet.

With so many gangsters and associate gangsters and associated associates going around, it got a bit difficult to tell who was who and some gangs devised elaborate codes to tell gangs from one another. The codes included the colours of your clothes and the cigarettes you smoked (or choked on, if you were still in school). If you came from an area where the colour code was white and red and wanted to enter a territory where the accepted code was black and white, you were in for some visa problems. There was a good chance you'd be approached by some scouts from the rival gang and an equally good chance you'd be chased or bashed up if you gave either the right or wrong answers.

Anyway, the sixties were an exciting time because it was then that the cops began to have the upper hand. The country's leading gangsters were exiled to an offshore penal settlement called Pulau Senang ("Isle of Ease") and the minions in the lower echelons were harrassed out of existence. By the end of the sixties, gangsterism had ceased to be a scourge. I believe drugs took over in the seventies but that's not my business here.

If I may be allowed an indulgence here, I would like to observe that the sixties probably saw the most exciting era in music ever. For it was in this period that

Singapore schoolboys began to take to the stage, imitating the music of groups like the Shadows, the Beatles and the Rolling Stones. Television had not been introduced in Singapore yet and what Singaporean fans wanted were Singapore replicas of their favourite international artistes. Contests were regularly held to discover Singapore's Elvis Presley, Cliff Richard, Paul Anka, and the Beatles, among many others.

Pop concerts always drew huge crowds and the largest venue, the Singapore Badminton Hall, drew as many as 10,000 per show. The atmosphere was stifling, the sound equipment hideously inadequate and the acoustics ghastly but the raucous din never failed to draw lusty encores as well as lusty boos. Those were the days, I hasten to add, when courtesy campaigns didn't exist.

Recording companies in Singapore recognised that somewhere in the middle of all those electric soundstorms there was talent waiting to be exploited and they moved in quickly. Within the first five years of the sixties, most local groups that could bash out music in harmony and in time were on one record label or the other.

But the sixties were not an era of affluence, by any means, and few teenagers could afford to buy records, least of all record players. Cassette players hadn't arrived yet. Any group that could sell more than 5,000 EPs (45 rpm Extended Play records, now of interest only to archaelogists) was considered A Big Deal.

But Big Deal and Big Time were two different things. I know of one recording artiste who rushed into town upon hearing that his half-yearly record royalties were due and collected $3.20, which was just enough to get him home by taxi.

But any hopes that an artiste might have had of making it big money wise were dashed by the entry of pirate record manufacturers who began by duplicating their records and then producing mongrel albums with the top songs from various other albums. The same musician who collected $3.20 in royalties remarked that the only consolation he got out of the pirate situation was that his song was included on the same album as songs from the Beatles, Tom Jones and the Supremes.

But living was cheap in the sixties. Maybe every generation claims that distinction nostalgically but the sixties were unique in that it was okay to be poor and to be seen to be poor. Five bucks could still give a teenager and girlfriend a reasonable time, covering a cinema ticket, bus fares and a soft drink. If you added a dollar to the budget, you could probably have a milk shake in an air-conditioned snack bar with a menu to read. For a little more money (or if you had the nerve to let your date share the cost), you could always go to a Sunday tea-dance. Sunday tea-dances were held in nightclubs and pubs mainly in the Orchard Road area spilling occasionally into the east coast suburbs. For a couple of dollars each, you could buy yourselves three hours of dancing time with a Coke thrown in. It was a pleasant way to spend a Sunday afternoon even for the fellows who couldn't organise a date. Unfortunately many of the fellows who couldn't organise a date would come along to the tea dances to organise other fellows' dates and this time bottles of Coke could

really get thrown in and across dance floors. Towards the end of the sixties, drug peddlers began to show up at tea dances too, adding a sleazy touch to the whole scene. The government decided that tea dances were an undesirable social activity and closed them down promptly. End of one era.

But the music scene was by no means strangled by the restrictions. Restrictions were nothing new to many young musicians who had seen Elvis Presley's music "discouraged" for three years over radio, juke box parlours and rock n'roll banned outright and people with long hair officially ostracised. Other more exciting things were happening — sophisticated dance-clubs were springing up all over Singapore looking for full-time musicians who could play the latest hits. Young musicians with poor academic qualifications and few prospects in life found they could now turn professional, earn good money and command a lot of respect from their family and friends. Writing and recording songs took second place to duplicating top twenty material in posh clubs. The creative element in local music that had been born in in the sixties disappeared in the sixties, succumbing to a commercialism from which it has not recovered.

Musicians and other symbols of "decadent cultures" weren't the only ones to feel government pressure in the early sixties. The political scene itself was an explosive one brought about by clashes between the government and a militant, leftist opposition and by military confrontation provoked by President Sukarno in Indonesia. It was in the sixties too that young students such as myself switched citizenships thrice, from being British subjects to being Malaysians to being Singaporeans.

But the most conspicuous difference between Singapore in the sixties and Singapore today is undoubtedly a physical one, brought about by the complete transformation of the cityscape.

If you look at the sprawling housing estates that confront you in all directions in Singapore, where nearly 85 per cent of the population reside, you mustn't forget that they began to sprout only in the sixties and proliferated in the seventies. In the sixties, most of the population still lived in villages or slums or compound houses paying paltry rents. Most houses didn't have piped water but many communities had a public standpipe which served as a kind of modern village well. Men and women bathed there, manoeuvring their towels and sarongs deftly to preserve their modesty, carting off water in kerosene tins later, for use in their kitchens.

If you lived in a compound house with piped water, you were luckier but only if you didn't have to share the house with ten others. Coming from a large family, as was the case with most Singapore families in the pre-family planning era, I remember what a hassle it was lining up to use the single bathroom in the house. The bathroom and kitchen areas always looked like some kind of refugee camp with forlorn family members wandering around brandishing toothbrushes and towels cheerily labelled "Good Morning".

Nowadays, as I join my brother, his wife and their two sons for breakfast in their five-room government flat with not one but three places where they can comfortably brush their teeth, I always envy the kids for having their own bathrooms. Twenty five years ago, that lovely park which their flat overlooks was a swamp with the occasional crocodile wandering through. The farmers living in it felt so isolated that they

195

referred to travelling to the city as journeying "to Singapore". Now it takes my brother less than twenty minutes to make that trip across the expressways in his Toyota.

His Toyota. In 1962 when we were discussing motorcycles, and names like Triumph, BSA, Norton and Ariel were being mentioned in hushed tones of veneration, one fourteen-year old told us his brother owned a Honda. "What's that?" exclaimed the motorbike expert in our midst.

"What's that?" asks my nephew when I mention radios called Grundig and Blue Spot, cars called Simcas, Holdens, Cortinas and Austins, watches called Titus, Roskopf and Favre-Leuba, cigarettes called Craven A, Clock Tower and Winning Rush, cinemas called Roxy, Alhambra, Pavilion and Majestic and pop groups called Sam the Sham and the Pharoahs of "Woolly Bully" fame.

Standing at the junction of North Bridge Road and Stamford Road facing Raffles City, I have the new Singapore in front of me and the old Singapore behind me in the form of the glorious old Capitol Cinema. The snack bar is still there serving malted milk shakes. And the long, dark gallery leading to the cinema proper is still there, lined with posters and mirrors.

When "grease" was the word, even in the sixties, that gallery was always full of skinny but dapper teenagers meticulously combing their oily hair in front of those mirrors. "Brylcreem" was synonymous with style in those days, even though the oily, yoghurt-like mixture came in large glass jars shaped like vases.

One of the most popular cinema ads in those days was the Brylcreem ad. One version began with a diver jumping off a diving board. Halfway down, the camera freezes and closes up on his face.

"*Apa pasal*? (What happened?)" says the narrator. "*Saya suda lupah saya punya Brylcreem* (I have forgotten my Brylcreem)" says the diver, and the film reverses rapidly showing him backtracking to the diving board. Grease is out these days and so are a great many other things. But I hope I won't ever have to say "*Saya sudah lupah saya punya sixties.*"

Kampung: A Familiar Place
by Sharifah Hamzah

I step gingerly on the creaking planks, looking for any remnant of identity, any interesting curio of life in this abandoned, dismantled kampung house.

I find a photograph of a young man; his torn, rain-soaked magazines and dairies lie scattered at my feet. I feel like an intruder and yet I feel that I know him because we have shared a common experience.

Twenty years ago, I had stood under a tree and watched my own kampung house being bulldozed into oblivion, leaving behind my family's own trail of photographs, broken crockery and paraphernalia of living.

At one time, most Malay families lived in kampungs — villages. But the term encompasses more. It represents a distinct community concept which stretches way back into the history of the Malay Archipelago.

Early pioneers established settlements along waterfronts and on fertile land; creative small communities bonded not only by similar ambitions but also by a strong instinct for survival and independence.

Malay folklore has full-blooded accounts of warriors who fought off mischief-makers bent on disturbing the peace of his kampung.

With modernization, kampungs were progressively replaced with other residential alternatives. Today, the few remaining kampungs in Singapore face a temporary future as urban development is likely to completely do away with them by the end of the decade.

My family lived in a small kampung in the Geylang district near the East Coast of Singapore. There, the dwellings of thirty Malay households and a sprinkling of Chinese and Indian families nestled together into a hamlet.

Our family home was built by Grandfather, and when he died an early death, Grandmother brought up her eleven children under its sheltering roof. My cousins and I were its third generation of occupants.

As there were so many of us, it was fortunate that Grandfather built a large house on a spacious piece of land.

In fact, the site is now occupied by four terrace houses!

The architecture of the kampung house is ingeniously adapted to tropical climate. Most, including my own, are built of wood, raised on stilts and have pitched roofs.

The stilts elevate the house about 1.5 metres above ground to prevent moisture from seeping through the cool wooden floorboards. But we found other uses for this space between floor and earth.

My family stored bicycles and bric-a-brac under the house. When we played hide and seek as children, it was a faithful standby whenever other good hiding places had been taken. And after a scolding, I would take my anger and self-pity for a quiet moment in the embryonic space to emerge ready for the world again.

Architects admire the logic behind the pitched kampung roofs. Their high ceilings are ideal for inducing ventilation and the design facilitates rapid runoff of rain water. The latter I can vouchsafe, because whenever it poured, my childhood friends and I would take turns standing under the eaves enjoying the cool, hard-hitting 'waterfall' on our backs.

A typical kampung house usually consists of three main parts: the *beranda* (verandah), the *rumah ibu* (main house) and the *rumah dapur* (kitchen section). The *rumah ibu* of our home was divided into the *serambi* or reception area and the *ruang tengah*, a wide passageway, flanked by bedrooms, which led to the kitchen.

Each area had a specific function, but there was much flexibility. It seems quite marvelous now as I recall the ways we used to adapt our rooms to different needs and demands.

According to the Muslim code of propriety, the entertainment of guests is based on the segregation of sexes. So, when a mixed group of visitors arrive, males would normally be ushered to the *beranda* while the ladies chatted in the *serambi*.

Kenduri or a feast where prayers are shared to celebrate or bless an important occasion is quite often held in a kampung. On such

occasions, the number of neighbours and relatives invited would be so large that it takes some ingenuity to fit everyone into the house. In those circumstances, rooms were easily adapted to fit the purpose.

Such flexibility is quickly achieved because dining Malay style is *sans* furniture: everyone sits on the floor in two rows facing each other and the food is laid out between them. In large celebrations the men would be served in the *serambi* while the ladies had their meal along the *ruang tengah*.

Then when the family holds the grandest affair — a wedding celebration — neighbours and relatives would come to help with the preparations, and some would certainly stay overnight. At such times, members and close friends of the family would use the *serambi* as a communal sleeping area, leaving honoured guests the use of the bedrooms.

Even in the absence of celebrations, every room of our house evoke many memories of my youth and childhood.

The *beranda* was the family recreational centre, especially on balmy afternoons. My uncles, mostly dressed in nothing more than sarongs, sat crossed legged and played *dam* (checkers). In one corner, Grandmother would be seated with her *sireh* box, spreading a betel leaf with slaked lime and shavings of areaca nut and gambier, casually folding the combination into a neat packet and popping it into her mouth. She always enjoyed the pleasure of chewing this mildly stimulating Malay 'tobacco'. In another corner, next to my pet mynah, my best friends and I would sit playing five stones or some private game.

When I was ten, I fancied myself to have a great talent in badminton. In the afternoons, when friends were not always available to play, I would turn to the adults. But it was almost impossible to coax them out into the bright, hot sunlight. What could one do?

Why, turn the *ruang tengah* into a make shift badminton court, of course. Running on formica and surrounded by planks walls, I learnt new strokes and imagined myself a budding Thomas Cup star.

Most kampung homes have a side-door in the kitchen and it is the custom that female guests prefer to announce their arrival at this entrance rather than the main one.

At home, this side door was also the venue of our daily tea. Around 4 p.m. we would gather there to chat and look out for itinerant (cake) hawkers who, depending on who passed our way first, would determine the afternoon's menu.

The extended family is the norm rather than the exception in every kampung. Young and old live under one roof, and it is customary that when a daughter married, she and her husband would make her family house their home, beginning another generation to ensure its continuing occupancy.

Being part of such a family prepares an individual for his role in the kampung community, for it is a very closed knit one.

Everyone knows everybody, and neighbours, after years of social and emotional contact, assume the standing of blood relations.

The spirit of *gotong royong* — of helping one another — is not only confined to physical support in the construction of houses, maintenance of the *surau* (mosque) or the organization of community celebrations. Families share each other's sorrow and happiness. The old hold a venerable position and youth seek the wisdom of age.

In such an environment, the western concept of privacy is alien.

In a society where personal links with the community is so tightly woven, it is more difficult for an individual to assert his independence not to say adopt ideas or lifestyles that deviate from the accepted ways.

And if he did, he opened himself to scrutiny and criticism from both family and neighbours.

Perhaps it was someone who had been given to such exasperation, who coined the saying *'jaga tepi kain orang'*, 'watch over the matters of another from the length of your sarong.' Meaning: keep a discreet distance; a piece of advice directed at those who indulge in being busy-bodies.

But the identification of the individual with his kampung is strong. Malay songs and poems, when they tell of a traveller's yearning for familiar ground, inevitably sigh: *'rindukan kampung halaman'* — missing my kampung and not home.

And is it surprising that socialization starts early in the kampung? As most kampung games which children play are team games, sooner or later, even the shyest child will creep out of his shell and find a play-group to join. Perhaps his brothers, sisters or cousins would initiate him into a 'gang'.

I had good friends in my kampung and we didn't need many toys; there was so much to explore and we had each other.

An unused chicken coop became the group's headquarters though it was only big enough for two to squeeze in at a time. A second-hand pink bathtub which my father introduced to the family was quickly relegated to the backyard to become a boat which took us on journeys across the frontiers of fantasy. Poor Father, we all preferred the time-tested 'scoop and splash' method of bathing.

SINGAPORE SLING

We also learnt to fly kites and prepare the lethal glass strings for kite battles.

To make this glass-coated string, we needed a chemical which we bought from petrol stations (never knowing what it was called, we just pointed), a quantity of broken glass, two trees which stood close together and a spool of mother's thread.

First, we heated the chemical to a sticky consistency, and added the glass which we had carefully pounded. Then, using a length of wire, the roll of thread was soaked in the substance, but not before tying one end of the thread to a tree. This allowed us to wind the treated thread around the trees to dry into a razor-edged twine.

Then a battle was waged in the air. The kites dodged and swooped as the fliers positioned them to cut the opponent's kite string with the treated thread. Once severed, the losing kite would drift away, setting off another battle among other children who raced away to retrieve the fallen kite.

My first nature lessons were held in our garden even before I started school: shy mimosas that folded their leaves when touched, wild fruits that popped when pressed and sweet nectars of flowers which you could suck all held new fascination.

There were also two jambu trees and guava and jackfruit trees around our house, which meant there was always fresh fruit to be plucked and enjoyed.

As for food in general, there was much more to buy and try without wandering too far from home.

In the afternoons, boys from our kampung and neighbouring ones plied the shaded lanes with a variety of sweet and savoury cakes, calling their wares.

When an enterprising neighbour bought a refrigerator, she froze fruit juices and syrups in narrow plastic bags, and sold them to eager young customers. We enjoyed this ice lolly, chewing off a corner of the bag and sucking the cool refreshment straight into our throats. She called her treat *Air Batu Malaysia* — Malaysian Ice.

But she could never beat the popularity of Kadir the ice seller.

Whenever he arrived with his cart, we kampung children would all crowd around him, shouting our orders for ice balls.

It was a joy in itself to watch him shave the block of ice with his ice shaver, eloquently moulding the shavings into a ball with his bare hands and dribbling red, green, blue and yellow syrup onto the cold treat.

Some time ago, when I recalled old growing-up times with my kampung friends, the subject of our favourite hawker was naturally brought up.

We had all, it seems, noticed that bad sore on Kadir's finger which never seemed to heal but with the reckless bravado of the young, we had dismissed it as an insignificant detail or pretended that we didn't see!

In spite of the tranquil, unspoilt setting of kampung life, it would be unrealistic to imagine that it was without disadvantages.

There was that 'bucket system', the neither hygienic nor convenient form of sanitation which required the buckets used for collecting human effluent to be replaced manually every day.

The toilets smelt and were almost always away from the house, which meant that when nature called in the night, you had to pick your way through the darkness to the outhouse by the slender beam of a torchlight. And since most households had only one toilet, there was also often the inconvenience of a queue.

Today, the majority of Singapore Malays have been resettled in government-built flats equipped with every modern convenience.

However, a flush toilet is but a small consolation.

When the first families were uprooted from their homes, they must have felt as bewildered as the deer of the Malay saying which strayed into a kampung.

Three-, even four-generation families had to be broken up, life-long neighbours parted ways, fruit trees and lovingly tended gardens were left behind. It was a painful farewell for ever.

But kampung-folk adjusted to high-rise living and strangely the old kampung ways eased the transition.

Friends, many floors up or blocks away, would still extend the same familiar kampung friendship, renewing the spirit of neighbourhood and establishing real links rare in the world of pigeon-hole living.

So, though the day will come when kampungs in their tangible form disappear altogether from the face of Singapore, its essence and the values which it shelters, will withstand, as the pitched roof of a kampung house parries rain, the torrents of change and time.

CONFESSIONS OF A FOODIE
by Violet Oon

EVERYONE imagines that as food critic I get to eat the best food in town. Yet I often wonder if this is true.

That's because the first thing anyone says on discovering a gem of a restaurant or hawker-stall is: "Don't you dare tell Violet Oon. She'll write about it and then the prices will go up and the standards down.

"It'll be death to the place."

So my job is a pretty difficult one, akin to that of a spy's. The hunt's on daily for the best and the brightest, aided fortunately by some gourmands who cannot resist boasting that they were the first to make a find.

Yes, I'm not the only one to make a profession in Singapore out of eating and spending time chasing that elusive best fish-head curry, char kway teow or yew char kway.

Sometimes if an out-of-towner happens upon a conversation about food, usually taking place during a meal, he'll think that most Singaporeans are food pro-fessionals rather than the lawyer, engineer or doctor that they are in real life.

Could it be that perhaps real life is the passionate pursuit of fine food while the business of doctor-ing, lawyering and engineering is simply a part-time necessary evil to finance the eating forays?

In a nutshell the typical Sing-aporean is one who devotes entire chunks of his lifetime to eating; breakfast, morning coffee, lunch, tea, a pre-dinner snack, dinner and then at 1 a.m., to round off the day — supper.

We live to eat and do not quite eat to live. There's no such thing as a simple meal for the Singapo-rean. Every feast comes close to a production number.

For most Singaporeans the per-formance of eating should prefer-ably be conducted out of the house. We prefer having someone else slave over producing our ambroisiac meal.

Besides eating, another entire chunk of a lifetime is spent on the hunt — the chase sometimes is even more exciting than the quarry.

Because if there's one thing that beats eating, it's the discovery of a new exciting place for food.

To be the first to discover a good restaurant is as heady as striking oil in your backyard.

The pleasure is heightened if the new place discovered is as difficult as is possible to locate and with a name as unpronounceable as can be.

Thus it is that one of the most prestigious of dining experiences is to be found in Sembawang, in the deepest of Singapore's rural land.

I have never eaten in this place, a restaurant without a name, off a road without a sign and with opening hours that are erratic.

Apparently the French couple who run the place opens the restaurant when they feel like it.

I did toy with the idea once of eating there but when the directions included turning left at a particular tree and hitting a dirt track, I gave up.

A true gourmet will accuse me of not being made of the right stuff and showing true grit.

Singaporeans eat with a passion but exactly what do we put into our mouths?

A "rojak" of foods is the best description. We go Chinese, Malay, Indian, Italian, French, Thai and American at will — McDonald's for breakfast, Prego's for lunch, perhaps a roti prata or two at Jalan Kayu for tea and the Whitley Road Food Centre for dinner.

Oftentimes we mix and match several food traditions at one meal, taking a bite of char kway teow (Chinese fried noodles) between sticks of satay in peanut sauce (Malay kebabs) and washing it all down with a piping bowl of soup kambing (Indian mutton soup).

What's the taste like? A delicious mixture of gutsy spiciness from cloves, cardamons, cinnamon, turmeric, ginger, shrimp paste, with the edge taken off by mellow rich coconut milk. Then there's the different appeal of Chinese tastes imparted by soya sauce, bean pastes, rice wine, sesame oil and oyster sauce.

In other words, variety is our spice of life.

Not only does the food taste good. Eating out in Singapore is like attending a play or concert with the players producing a fugue of sounds, action and colour enough to rival the best military tattoes or even the closing ceremony of the Los Angeles Olympics.

First the look. The blandness of fish in white sauce — non colour, or hospital inspired sterile display of food is not for us Singaporeans. The artist in us emerges most with food. The lovingly displayed pyramids of fruits or raw seafood and vegetables in a hawker stall pleasures your eyes before you even get to taste a morsel.

Then the drama of actually seeing your food prepared and cooked whets your appetite even more.

The Roti Prata man throws his sheet of dough in the air in perfectly coordinated dance-like movements. This drama is so important to the taste of the prata that the dish does not really appeal when it's eaten at home in a takeaway plastic bag.

The total taste sensation falls flat.

As it does when you don't actually hear the char kway teow seller clanging his ladle against the side of his wok (music to our ears) or see the tea being "pulled" from glass to glass in "teh tarek."

Who says that there's nothing for the tourist or overseas visitor to see in Singapore?

I find that nothing fascinates them more than the skill of the sarabat man who literally pulls a glass of boiling hot tea into another forming a perfect armslength arc of suspended liquid. "Will it spill or won't it?" They wait with bated breath to see if this magic can be pulled off.

I've often had to pay the sarabat man for five glasses of tea or coffee at a go so that visiting photographers can take pictures of this gravity defying feat.

The theatre of food is not only found in hawker stalls. Our poshest of restaurants also indulge in high drama.

One of the most exciting meals to be had is to sit on the top floor of the Shangri-la Hotel at the Nadaman Japanese Restaurant. Here, against the backdrop of the Singapore skyline, you watch the Japanese chef perform some nifty tricks with his knife and ladle as he cooks teppanyaki for you. His exacting performance brings envy to the eyes of the best of Ninjas.

And attending a Chinese wedding dinner is also very much like attending your son's passing out parade in the army.

The guests, many of whom have already been sitting patiently for over an hour for the bride to arrive, perk up when the lights go off and the swinging doors from the kitchen open with a swoosh to disgorge with military precision drilled troops of waiters carrying aloft large silver platters of food, parading to the tune of "The Colonel Bogey March" from *The Bridge of the River Kwai*.

I don't know if the choice of music has a deeper psychological meaning but this stirring entrance of glorious food after such a long wait usually draws an appreciative round of spontaneous applause.

This is tribute indeed from the Singaporean because he seldom breaks into spontaneous applause for anything. Concert artistes and the greats of the pop world have often wondered at our reticence.

Some hotels have gone even further in their overture to the first course of a Chinese banquet.

At the Tai-Pan, the lights go out and waiters come in bearing torches to the throb of the theme from *Star Wars*.

Psychedelic lights are the order of the day here.

Yes, lights do play an important part in the business of food.

Even before lighting consultancy became the "in" thing for our elegant restaurants, the traditionalists knew what it was all about.

Some hawkers take a leaf out of Hollywood and string naked bulbs round their stalls very much the way naked bulbs are set round the mirrors in the dressing rooms of the Hollywood star. The aim's the same — to highlight the star — in this case the food.

When it comes to a festive season, lights play an even more important role. The Moon Cake Festival sees a quiet byway like Mosque Street rival the brightness of Las Vegas. Colourful lanterns are strung round the sides and tops of shop fronts, which are given even more colour by the lurid billboard paintings framing the shops.

Some restaurants take great pride that the eyes of the dragon (carved out of a giant carrot) which decorates a dish actually lights up and blinks with battery power.

Now you know the origin of the term "theatre restaurant".

Where should we actually eat? Chinese food is of course the dominant kitchen in Singapore because most Singaporeans are Chinese ethnically.

The Cantonese restaurant tradition has always been strong. My favourites are the old style Spring Court in New Bridge Road where service and decor are fine but not particularly stylish. But the food's the thing there.

For more elegant dining, opt for the Summer Palace in the Pavilion Inter-Continental where I always feel as though I'm eating in a Shanghai bordello of the 1930s with its pink ruched fabric screens.

The Shang Palace of the Shangri-la serves some pretty delicious food and is a nice place to entertain during lunch — its dim sum provides a budget meal in posh surroundings.

Hong Kong new wave restaurants are represented by the Tung Lok in Liang Court and the newer Full Moon in the Glass Hotel.

Sometimes I like to go Teochew and then my two haunts are the Chao Zhou Garden in UIC Building and the Feng Cheng Lou in Crown Prince Hotel. Both serve exquisitely delicate food but at quite a high price.

Be prepared to spend at least $30 per head if you want a satisfactory meal.

The Hokkiens are the largest Chinese dialect group in Singapore yet there are very few Hokkien restaurants around.

Beng Thin is still the most well known while Beng Hiang runs a close second. Near the Beng Hiang is another favourite restaurant of mine — the Moi Kong which serves Hakka food.

This is more peasant cuisine and totally different from the usual Cantonese fare. I love the dishes they make out of the home made red rice wine for which the Hakkas are well-known.

The Mooi Chin used to be in the Hainanese heartland near Raffles Hotel but it is now in Ang Mo Kio and devilishly difficult to locate.

There, Hainanese food is the order of the day — a combination of wholesome cooking with influences from Nonya and English food. At the old restaurant, the stewed ox tongue was out of this world but unfortunately it's no longer part of the regular menu.

Mix the relative blandness of Chinese food with the spiciness of Malay food and you have Nonya cuisine. They make exciting meals and today's most visable repository of this kind of food is at Peranakan Place in Emerald Hill Road.

I rather enjoy going instead into the heartland of Baba culture in Katong and eating at the Guan Hoe Soon restaurant in Joo Chiat Road.

Talking of Malay food, it was, till recently, very much a home style affair, like Nonya food. You could only get the best in the homes of friends.

Today the two classy Malay restaurants that have brought home cooking to us hungry hordes are Aziza's in Emerald Hill Road and the Bintang Timur in Far East Plaza.

Now to the Indian part of Singapore's food.

When I was a child, the most famous eating out place for Indian food was the Islamic Restaurant in North Bridge Road.

They're a shadow of their former selves but the Islamic and the Zam Zam, Singapore and Victory Restaurants in the vicinity still enjoy a regular clientele for their offerings of murtabak, Nasi Briani and fish curry.

Be forewarned that these are old style restaurants, without air-conditioning and are more like coffee shops.

Today, eating Indian has become a more sophisticated affair. Northern Indian food has become chic and top tables are to be found at the Tandoor Restaurant at the Holiday Inn Parkview and the Rang Mahal of the Oberoi Imperial Hotel.

These provide fine food as well as service and ambience.

Many of the younger Singaporeans are completely unaware of the Omar Khayyum in Hill Street, opposite the American Embassy but it was the first Northern Indian restaurant in Singapore and was once the most exciting place for expatriates.

Less chic but very comfortable Northern Indian restaurants are the Mumtaz Mahal in Far East Plaza where the decor is plain but the service and food very fine, the Mayarani in Boulevard Hotel and the famed Moti Mahal in Food Alley off Maxwell Road.

The word "mahal" means expensive in Malay and many diners feel that it describes Northern Indian food to perfection.

Finally the type of Indian eating that has caught on firmly among Singaporeans is the "banana leaf style" eating where food is served on banana leaves and the curries are fiery hot.

The speciality of the house is always Fish Head Curry and you make eyeball to eyeball contact with the fish you're eating.

Do you know that Race Course Road has turned into a sort of curry street? This was a very natural development being only a street away from Little India. Eating there is great fun.

en fried in soya sauce.

One famous curry restaurant that's not in the news but a favourite with older gourmets is found along Selegie Road opposite Selegie Complex. Again this is Indian curry cooked by Chinese and the open fronted shop front is so narrow that you'll miss it completely when you're driving past.

The food is served only during

The two famous names in the street are Muthu's Curry which was the original curry-shop there and the Apollo Banana Leaf. There is also Indian curry cooked by Chinese in the coffee shop called Soon Heng.

At the Soon Heng there's a fun mix of the pungency and gutsiness of Indian curries contrasting completely with the flavours of chick-

lunch and in the 1970's, a never ending stream of be-jewelled "tai-tais" would disgorge from their chauffeur-driven Mercedes Benzes with tiffin carrier in each hand to buy fish head and other assorted curries for their mahjong party luncheons.

If you're obsessed with comfort, taking home the food rather than eating it in these poorly

ventilated coffee shop restaurants would be a compromise. These places make no concessions to your comfort.

The food's wonderful but you sweat your way through the meal. But we Singaporeans are hardy types. At these famous shop restaurants you'll find nifty executives in long shirt sleeves and ties eating cheek by jowl with the taxi driver, both of them completely oblivious of the stiffling heat and discomfort.

I always feel that I've been through a sauna after one of these meals.

But perhaps my daughter has got it right.

One night we were sweating it out with a few hundred other people outside that famous steamboat restaurant in Ang Mo Kio called Sea King. It's back to back with Avenue 6 and near the Court's Furniture Store and Jack's Garden Restaurant.

Thought I aloud: "We're silly fools eating this winter food in the summer heat of Singapore."

Piped up my nine-year-old: "Mummy, I don't know why but I really enjoy eating steamboat here. Sometimes we go to an air-conditioned restaurant but it's just not the same.

"Not so much fun Mummy. When it's air-conditioned I don't feel as though I've really eaten anything after it all."

It's just like a game of tennis or squash. When you sweat it all out, there's that feeling of satisfaction which comes after strenuous physical exercise.

But we can't fool ourselves into thinking that all those calories imbied were being burned up during the meal.

Eating al fresco, though, need not always be a strenuous physical effort. Because, it's not always hot and the breezes are most refreshing.

Hawker-style eating is still most fun because the food's not only good, it's cheap.

If there're four people eating together, $5 each buys a wonderful variety of food — a mix of Chinese, Malay, Indian and even "western".

Every hawker centre now boasts of a "western" grill stall and even some simulation of the American fast foods — like a hamburger or hot dog.

In case you do not know, the whole of Singapore is dotted with hawker centres. These hawkers used to ply the streets with their food until they were made to stay put for the convenience of food hunters.

The rule of thumb here is — anything goes.

Sit anywhere you like and then place your orders with any or every stall. Then just sit and wait, relax and a whole army of servers will bring your food to you.

Because the food's inexpensive, it's not money but the size of the table that will restrict your choice.

When the food arrives, the thing to do is to share. Everyone takes a bite out of every dish.

If you're fussy about your territory try getting one of the hawkers to serve you with individual bowls or small side plates. Then pile the food onto that.

This 'anything goes' mentality has also spilled onto our formal restaurant eating.

No self-respecting gourmet will eat only what he or she has ordered in an European meal. If there are four people eating together, the thing to do would be to order twelve completely different dishes to make up the three courses for each person and then to have a bite of the food ordered by your companions. We all like to have a taste of something different.

So when your $50 bill for your three dishes comes, you pay for three but you've actually eaten twelve. Doesn't this make much more sense?

So as I prepare to tuck into yet another meal, I wish you the best in eating and remember to let the gypsy in you take over when it comes to food.

Be adventurous, be innovative and please only yourself.

A-E-I-O-U
Abroad / Eating / Invited / Office / Urbanised
by Toh Paik Choo

COMMUTER chat, lovers' lingo, officialese, parent parley, student speak, travel talk, complex communicate. Call it by any other name as it is bandied islandwide and it still comes home as Singlish, the hybrid lingua peculiar to Singapore (and Malaysia). And it goes far beyond just ending an articulation on a "lah" note, nor is it expressly confined to the slanguage alone as this primer will show.

WHEN IN ROME, DO LIKE HOME

Whoever it was who said there are only two ways to travel — with children and without — never travelled with the Singaporean, obviously, and hence has not lived to record the third experience.

Up Country / Out Station is not a succinct protest march by our pig and paddy farmers against our mass rapid transport. It is the colonial-dated but still used expression (more by the older generation) for "travelling." Going "up country" and "out station" is to leave Singapore either for business or pleasure. "Taking a trip..." is more up-to-date.

No Morning Sun may sound like the start to a folksong chorus but is really a phrase that has fazed many a frontdesk person in many a hotel abroad. "Ah Choo,* tell the clerk my room don't want morning sun." Here the speaker requests that the windows of his hotel room do not receive the early rays of sunlight which normally herald the break of day. Reason? "Frighten hot."

Frighten hot, Frighten cold — "Frighten" in this vernacular does not

---

* All first-syllable Chinese names can be dropped and replaced with "Ah" in a show of familiarity or affection or humour or contempt.

217

have the same meaning as that which appears on a cinema poster for a horror show. The Singlish "frighten" is a simile for "cannot stand" or "intolerable." In Greece, "frighten hot," in Switzerland, "frighten cold." Then why go? "Frighten people say never go anywhere."

Eat Until Frighten — Someday a Singapore hotel is going to promote the buffet to end all buffets with this line. Until that happens, here's how you're likely to hear it: "Don't tell me all our breakfasts like that? Every day bread, eat until frighten." The Singapore Tourist in alarm and disbelief at how anyone can function on a breakfast of a crusty roll. In this instance, the "frighten" is of terrifying proportions, brought on by fear of yet another noodle-less breakfast.

Hot Water / Take Medicine — Hot water may be what you take your bath in, but for the Singaporean Abroad, hot water is what you carry in a tupperware in a Yaohan plastic bag through eight cities in 15 days. For drinking, ("donno their water can drink or not") and for taking medicine.

Got chillie? Here where got chillie one? — Hot water may help the medicine go down but asking for chillie to go with the spaghetti will make the chef cry. Spoilt Singaporean: "Can ask they got chillie or not?" Slightly Sophisticated Singaporean: "Here where got chillie one?"

Don't mind to pay a bit more — Between the Spoilt and the Slightly Sophisticated you're bound to come up against the Show-off Singaporean. "Can ask them give more clams, less tomato, I'm sure we all don't mind to pay extra." Money spiaks, Singlish-style. "Spiaks" doubles for "speech" and "personality."

Tipsee / Kopi Money — From the newly-weds to the nearly-deads, nine out of ten Travelling Singaporeans do tip when reminded or encouraged to do so. "Tipsee" is Hongkong Chinese English (Chinglish) and "kopi (coffee) money" is localese, both refer to "gratuity."

Any discount? No free gift uh? — You can bank on the Singaporean to girdle the globe with this mantra never far from his lips, the whole idea of going on tour based on Annie Get Your Calculator's "Anything you can buy I can buy cheaper."

Instant Tell-Tale Singaporean Trait

On boarding a bus, at home and abroad, the true Son-of-Singapore never occupies an empty or just vacated space without first thumping the seat with his hand. Two answers: For reasons of hygiene, dust the seat. For reasons of health, sitting on a hot seat known to result in boils and blisters. There's a third answer but it's Peranakan and unprintable.

WE CAN'T GO ON TAKING LIKE THIS

When the host asks, "You take everything?" Speak up for your food allergies and religious taboos or forever hold your peace... at least until after the tenth course.

"Take" is "eat" and suggests a gentler motion than the carnivorous-sounding "eat" (much like "to ease oneself" for "to piss") though you wouldn't think so to look at our kamikazed after-dinner table.

Primarily heard in the Chinese community in these combinations:
"I never take cold drinks."
"I cannot take chocolate."
"I like to take plenty of vegetables."
"I don't take mutton."
"You dare to drink beer after taking durian."
"No good to take too much sugar."
"Feel like taking soup or not?"
"You better take more prawns, ha-ha."

Twice around the Chinese dinner table and you'll be a dab hand at the interpretations:
"I drink only warm water."
"It makes me break out in spots."
"I'm not crazy about flesh."
"Mutton stinks!"
"I subscribe to old wives' tales."
"I've been reading lately."
"Would you like to go for supper?"
"Private Singapore joke, nudge-nudge, wink-wink."

At other times (usually after the dining hours) you'll be asked, "Taken your breakfast/lunch/dinner?" Definitely considered much better form than the "hi-s" and the "hellos" which greeting it actually does represent. Nothing Freudian in this preoccupation with food and eating, just the fact that as the stomach is content, so too the person. And the correct response, whether or not you've had a bite in two days,

Instant Tell-Tale Singaporean Trait

How do you show the figure "six"? I used to think five fingers on the one hand plus the thumb of the other did the trick nicely until I started to notice more and more Singaporeans raising only the last finger and thumb (of a clenched fist) to denote six, sixty. Even economy has caught up with sign language. While the thumb is still employed to say all things number one, the index finger pointed at nose tip is used for "I" and "me". Watch closely the next time round the dinner table.

is "Just taken something, thanks," which is the same as saying, "I am very well, thanks."

Hardly a variation but there's also "**taken anything?**" from the friend who's concerned that you don't go hungry. If you "haven't taken anything all day," he'll insist you "take something first."

"Takeaway" foods have no relation with the Singlish "take."

And what of "eat?" Sure, it's common usage, especially by the young mother to child in supermarket, "No, boy, this one you don't know how to eat" — and from the old-elder to shop assistant, "This one how to eat?"

SLOWLY WALK / FREE COME OVER

Some bring trouble, others bring fruit in plastic bags, some others bring gossip and there are those who bring good cheer when they visit.

Visiting in Singapore is not as rigid as it is observed most elsewhere, given our lifestyle and comprehensive bus routes. Appointments can be left loose and there are no last trains to catch back to the suburbs.

For your next visit, brush up on this vocabulary:

Host: Come in, come in; sit, sit.

(Repetition to effect welcome, "sit" for "have a seat" or "do sit down.")

Guest: Disturbing you only.

(Polite visitor's defence mechanism, "disturbing" for "hope I'm not interrupting.")

Host: Can I fissue a drink?

("Fix you.")

Guest: Plain water can.

(Not plain water in a tin but "water will do." To ask for something fancy is not done, until host insists.)

Host: Came from work?

(Are you from the office?)

Guest: Have to pick up the churren from computer class afterword so I thought free might as well drop in.

Instant Tell-Tale Singaporean Trait

The excuse-me-stoop is not the latest in aerobicise but a move by over-considerate Singaporeans beating a path between a couple of people talking or a roomful of people listening to a speech or watching a slide show. Have you never spotted someone deliberately hunching herself as she makes her way before a row of audience at a talk so as not to cause distraction?

(Self-explanatory, including "churren" and "afterword.")
Host: Taken your...
(Have you had something to eat?)
Guest: Taken something at the office.
(For sure it wasn't an English grammar lesson)
Host: Don't be shy you know, sure you don't join me?
(An invitation to share host's meal)
Guest: Carry on, carry on, I also have to make a move.
(Thank you, no, you go ahead, it's time I leave anyway)
Host: Okay, Ban Ban Kia, Eng Lai Chay
(Slowly walk, free come over, or as they say in your neck of the woods, mind how you go and do pop by anytime.)

MY KERLIC OHSO

To expedite your overview of the following, within constraints, a prioritised broadbase has been consolidated in accordance with company policy... or can I get back to you? An exercise in "execucliches" heard the length and breadth of office blocks in Singapore. But if you listen attentively you'll be rewarded with this other kind of company conversation:

Order for me Toast Bread. — Breakfast on arrival in the office is not uncommon. "Toast bread" is common and is literally translated from dialect Chinese, because there's bread, and there's toast bread.

Off The Light / On The Light. — Where's the switch? It's been dropped, an example of spoken shortform (as opposed to written shorthand), here for "put on the light" and "switch off the light."

Go For Dinner — Another instance of verbal precis in Singapore. This could mean "the boss has left for dinner." It could also be a suggestion amongst colleagues "to eat out tonight."

My Kerlic Ohso — My colleague also... speaks like this?

Film sent for washing or not? — Taken from dialect Chinese "wash," term for "develop" or "process" of film. Precisely because the process of developing negatives into positives involves "washing."

Far-nee — Funny? Not at all in the least.

Computer Is Down — Breathes there a soul in Singapore who has not had these three words uttered to him?

An-ass — National Service abbreviated, example, "our office can apply an-ass deferment for you."

Ten-something — Works as well for time and cost, as in "em-dee always come in at ten-something,"(after 10 a.m.) and "our cost is already ten-something" (over $10).

From...? — All receptionists and secretaries have been programmed to say "from..?" immediately after you (the caller) have given your name.

YOU GIMME GOOD ONE / SWEET OR NOT?

It is not television that has killed conversation, far from it as every family with a resident kibitzer who cannot keep his running commentary to himself well knows. The "art of conversation" has been done in by supermarket shopping. Silent marketing, except for the rattle of trolley wheels, has sealed the fate of shoptalk as one picks, pays and returns to the carpark without even exchanging nine words with butcher, baker, cashier nor attendant.

Do you remember a time when shopping with your parents meant a half day's (which seemed like an eternity) traipsing up and down the North, South and New Bridge Roads and the High Street? Most of all, besides the Polar Cafe curry puffs break, do you remember your folks' bargain banter with the stallholders and shopkeepers?

Sweet Or Not? — All mummies have 'em! The knack for asking the fruit man if his oranges are sweet, papayas are ripe, melons are juicy. Not once was the man inconsistent; for 25 years he never wavered from "very sweet, very ripe, very juicy."

Gimme Good One Uh? — Having established the fruits' sterling properties mothers then conclude the buy with "you give me good one," not so much out of suspicion that he'll toss in a rotten apple but out of housewifely reflex action.

Can't Trust / Regular — When a mother then sinks her dentures into some sour grapes first reaction spat out is, "I told you don't buy from that fella, can't trust one. I always buy from my regular only."

Donno Real Or Bluff — Not a graduation to waxed fruits but to the shoe store we go. "Donno real or bluff" is how Mum expresses her sentiment over the pair of leather shoes you've chosen. She usually exits with the shoes and "sure not plastic ah" to the salesgirl.

Got New One? — After turning eight pairs out of their boxes, guaranteed she'll turn to the salesman and say, "Okay, this pattern, but give me new one." The smart salesman is the one who replies, "They are all new ones, one." The naive salesman rues the day he says, "In this pattern this one last pair" because that's when Ma seizes her opportunity, "Last pair? Then make it cheaper lah!" She got it too.

Fast Colour / Give Extra — Long before drip-dry and off-the-peg going to "cut cloth" (fabric shopping) was the norm. And no scissors got near a yard of material until it was conclusively proved that the cloth was "fast colour" (colour doesn't run), "wouldn't shrink" and "wouldn't crease." And when the sale was about to be sewn up you could count on Mother to add, "Gimme extra huh (couple of inches more), I always buy from you."

Instant Tell-Tale Singaporean Trait

Not tried, not tested, just blind faith, when you're out shopping with the folks. First to Bata, then to school. At Bata, oh, the ignominy of it all, a grown kid like you, having to ball up your fist while mother wraps the pair of socks round your hand. If the ankle meets the toe (of the socks) round your clenched fist, the sock'll fit.

The Roar of Singapore
by Kathleen Chopard

SHROUDED in the mist of the past is an ancient Malay legend about a famous, much honoured ruler from a land called Palembang, named Sri Tri Buana.

One day after braving a storm he and his nobles landed on an island with white, white sand called *Temasek*. They went hunting and suddenly saw in the distance, a strange creature with a red body, black head and white breast. It was powerfully built and moved with great speed. What is was nobody knew until someone said, "Your Highness, I have heard that in ancient times it was a lion that had that appearance..."

Sri Tri Buana who was in search of a site on which to establish a city, decided that he had found the perfect location and renamed the island *Singapura* or *Lion City*, a name that was in general use by the end of the 13th century.

As time passed, his descendents built a great city to which foreigners flocked in large numbers such that its fame soon spread far and wide.

But the history of the island goes back much further in time. Few Singaporeans, and even fewer foreigners, know that there exist historical records that provide evidence of the existance of old Singapore going back from the 13th century as far as the 3rd century.

Ancient Chinese texts mention *P'u Luo Chung*, the oldest known reference to Singapore. It was also called *Ma-Li-Yü R* in Mongol times and *Tan-Ma-Siak* in 1330. Admiral Cheng Ho, China's most famous navigator, referred to it as *Tan-Ma-Hsi* in the 15th century.

In Southeast Asia it was *Tumasek* or *Tumasik* (Sea Town). For more than 1700 years the island was the focus of trade routes between India and China but during the 14th century, the city was caught in the struggle between Siam (now Thailand) and

228

the Java-based Majapahit Empire. Shortly before 1400, Singapura was sacked and totally destroyed by the Javanese and the old settlement became a waste land, the site for the huts of Proto-Malayan sea-gypsies (Orang Laut) who were mostly pirates. Later, some Malay fisherfolk and a few Chinese farmers made the island their home.

This was what an Englishman, Thomas Stamford Raffles found in January 1819. Raffles had the foresight to see in Singapura, "a great commercial emporium," a "Free Port." In February of the same year, he planted the British Flag and so founded modern Singapore.

Raffles proved to be right for in a short space of time Singapore recaptured its former glory and became once more a thriving commercial port with a multi-racial population. It was ruled by the British until Singapore became a part of Malaysia on 16 September 1963.

On 9 August 1965, Singapore withdrew from Malaysia and became a sovereign, democratic and independent nation state.

The man responsible for the island passing from British to local hands was a youngish Prime Minister and Secretary-General of the ruling People's Action Party (PAP), a lawyer by profession, renowned for his brilliance, his acute powers of persuasion and his refreshing honesty. This man was Lee Kuan Yew (often refered to as LKY). He, together with a small but united group of dedicated associates, inherited an island of no more than 224 sq miles, populated by a multi-racial, multi-religious, multi-lingual, multi-cultural people, easily inflamed, given to rioting, living in slums. There was rampant unemployment and the population explosion only served to aggravate matters.

The government was made up of men who had been through hard times; they had fought the Communist and triumphed over colonialism. All of a sudden, without warning, they found themselves steering the ship of state under chaotic conditions with everyone rowing in different directions. The captain and his crew had to stabilise the floundering vessel and make for calmer waters. Their task was an unenviable one.

Armchair critics proclaimed that Singapore would go down the drain. Many of the English-educated fled the country. Those who remained either had nothing to lose or were like my parents who refused to panic. I remember my father saying to our many friends who were urging him to leave, "If the Japanese couldn't break my spirit, nothing else will and I believe in giving these chaps a chance." And so we remained.

Singapore's only assets were a hardworking people and its strategic location. With that tight-lipped tenacity that has seen him through many storms Lee and his dedicated team meticulously mapped out a plan for Singapore's future.

With a will the government set out to destroy the age-old racial divisions that made Singapore a human powder keg, ready to explode without warning. The British had unwittingly encouraged segregation in the belief that a people divided were easier to rule. As a result each community kept to itself, eyeing each other with mutual distrust, the English-educated having the advantage over the vernacular speaking groups.

It was vital that the smouldering barriers formed by a diversity of race, religion, language and culture be broken down. Lee Kuan Yew spoke of a people's government. It had, according to Lee, "to interpret its actions to four different audiences, each with its own scales and values." In order to meet them on their own terms, the English-educated Lee learnt Mandarin, Malay and Tamil.

Could Singapore succeed as an independent city state? The tentative steps at self-government taken by David Marshall and Lim Yew Hock in the 50s had come to nought. Singapore succeeded because it simply could not afford to fail. Lee himself must sometimes wonder at how quickly success came. But in reality he need not have feared because the people he was to lead were very much like himself — tough and equally determined to succeed because they had nowhere else to go. These were a migrant people used to a hard life. The many harsh unpopular policies Lee was forced to introduce over the years were to anger many but on the whole the people understood that there were no alternatives. Even those who hate Lee and his government respect him because he never took the soft option.

The first and probably most difficult task the government had to face was the clearance of the unsightly, unhygenic slums that grew out of the chaotic housing shortage. The rebuilding of Singapore had to be carefully planned and landscaped. Singapore has so little land and the decision was to build upward. Land reclamation schemes which added approximately 50 sq km, relieved some of the pressure.

Some people bemoan the clearing of the old parts of Singapore that have over the years made way for redevelopment. Once I took a group of foreigners for a walk through Chinatown pointing out the areas earmarked for demolision. One loud, indignant lady huffily exclaimed, "How can they destroy these quaint houses and colourful streets, these relics of the past!" Irritated because of her smug self-righteousness I turned to her, eyebrows raised and asked, "Dear, would you like to move into one of these dark, dank crowded tenements fronted by narrow, dingy streets?" She gaped, turned an unflattering shade of mottled crimson and promptly shut up. And so we heard no more of that.

Many people have accused the government of tearing down picturesque kampongs and villages and erecting faceless concrete jungles that resemble sterile phallic symbols reaching for the sky.

This is far from true. Each housing estate is specially designed to be a self-contained town complete with supermarkets, wet markets, cinemas, playgrounds, gardens and shops. They are crissed-crossed by efficient communication routes and can boast living standards second only to Japan.

Today 85 per cent of the population live in such flats and these are not boxes in the sky. Each house reflects the taste and culture of its occupant. People are living better and because they own their own flats have a stake in the country.

But all is not well. A new menace has reared its ugly head. Systematic eradication of the breeding grounds of mosquitoes and clean water had lessened the risk of malaria, dengue haemorrhagic fever, typhoid and cholera. Recently, however, a new and terrifying threat is stalking high-rise buildings. It can strike at any time, without warning, maiming, even killing its unsuspecting victims. This new threat is KILLER LITTER.

Over the years Singapore through its industrial programme and Five Year Plans achieved stability and became economically viable. From the air the first glimpse one gets as the plane makes its approach is the harbour dotted with hundreds of ships

Hair poster in vogue during the early 1970s.

MALES WITH LONG HAIR WILL BE ATTENDED TO LAST

LONG HAIR IS

| HAIR FALLING ACROSS THE FOREHEAD AND TOUCHING THE EYEBROWS | OR | HAIR COVERING THE EARS | OR | HAIR REACHING BELOW AN ORDINARY SHIRT COLLAR |

from all over the world. Just as many planes land at Changi International Airport daily.

On leaving the well-laid out airport terminal one may for a moment experience a blast of tropical heat but the trip to the city in one of Singapore's air-conditioned Comfort taxis is always interesting. Our taxi drivers are a politically aware lot and have a wry sense of humour. A first-time visitor was puzzled to learn that even lamposts wear *sarongs*. She soon discovered what he meant, travelling along wide roads lined by trees and colourful flowering shrubs that even found their way up the lamposts making them look like they were wearing flowered skirts. The garden city image is established from the first.

Talk of instant trees and travelling along roads that were once the sea also arouse interest and make for lively conversation.

Singapore is like a human patchwork quilt where Malays, Chinese, Indians and a host of others from East and West dwell harmoniously together. This is the magic that is Singapore today. Its success lies not in forcing every-one to be the same but in encouraging them to be different yet ensuring that they share the same goals and aspirations in an atmosphere of understanding and tolerance. Its strength is its differentness.

Not a month goes by without some festival being enthusiastically celebrated. Of the 11 public holidays each year, 9 are connected with one or another festival. These are colourful, delightful spectacles that locals never tire of being a part of. Foreigners stand entranced, bewitched, cameras click, a brow is wiped but everyone braves the heat. It is like drinking a cocktail, a cultural cocktail, the experience is heady, the senses reel, but you come back for more.

With economic prosperity and the rising standard of living peoples expectations have risen over the years. In the early years people's expectations have risen over bellies. Today, how one spends one's leisure has become important. It has been said that the only thing you can't do in Singapore is ski, but like one bright spark once said, "maybe the Government will build a huge dome around Bukit Timah Hill and refrigerate it and then we can ski. After all didn't we build the highest man-made waterfall in the world?" In Singapore nothing is impossible.

Singaporeans engage in a wide variety of indoor and outdoor activities. They walk, jog, bike, swim, skate, water ski, sail, fly. Martial arts, gymnastics, pugilistics and dance are popular and more recently health clubs and aerobics are gaining a following among the fashion-conscious younger generation.

Golf, tennis and badminton are a favourite with many and for those who prefer something indoors, there is yoga, chess, bowling and squash.

The interested observer may notice something about Singaporeans — they engage in recreation with the same dedication and determination they do everything else — with an eye on achieving excellence.

Not a day passes without at least one sale being advertised in the local papers.

And Singaporeans love them. We may not have mountains to

scale, rivers to ford, caves to explore but the suppressed excitement generated by sales makes up for this. People turn out in force, never so carefully was big game stalked; bodies tense, arms snake out, grabbing, feeling. Bargain hunters brave the heat, the rain, traffic snarls. They risk being shoved, crushed, the possibility of an elbow aimed at the ribs, even the excruciating pain of a heel to the instep.

Bargain hunters come in droves, they swarm around, thousands of people with a single purpose. They return home clutching plastic bags, satisfied with their prize, something that more often than not finds its way to the bottom of a storage cupboard.

Singapore is a land of campaigns. Cynical observers say that this is one other way the government has devised to generate additional income because heavy fines are levied against offenders. But do you remember what life was like before the campaigns?

It is an ancient Chinese belief that

Saliva is good
Phlegm is not
When in doubt
Spit it out!

Of course you got a warning, that discordant hawking sound but not everyone was lucky enough to get away in time. That drop of moisture that landed on you may not always have indicated the early arrival of the monsoon. And then there was NO SPITTING.

In the play, "She Stoops to Conquer," the future mother-in-law quizzed her daughter's prospective groom. She asks him if he smokes, he says yes. She approves saying that a young man should always have something to do with his hands.

It could have been this or all those ads telling the public that to be seen with a cigarette meant you had arrived. You were making a statement. So everyone between 18 and 80 lit up. Even the threat of cancer didn't deter many. Thousands smoked and loved ones, friends and members of the public were perpetually surrounded by a bluish-grey haze.

There was no convincing them that inhaling exhaled smoke was worse than actually smoking. Non smokers were in a typical Catch-22 situation. *Cancer if you do. Cancer if you don't.*

And then there was NO SMOKING. This applied to lifts, cinemas, public transport, government buildings, etc.

Being a migrant people, Singaporeans learnt early in life that to get ahead you had to climb to the top of the heap and they did, literally.

And then there was Q up.

People tended to think that streets were public disposal bins. No one cared about cleanliness. No one had heard of the Clean, Green, Garden City Concept.

And then there was NO LITTERING.

But these campaigns were easy to implement. The government's nemesis was how to control the population. "Control the population! They'll never succeed," exclaimed one cynical foreign wag, fat ciger in one hand and brandy snifter in the other. "What do you expect them to do after work, they have no recrea-tion, the poor buggers."

But this was the 60s and the problem went much deeper. The thinking in those days revolved around the more merrier!

Must have son, then can stop!

Then there was

Then like in Genesis it was said, "And the government saw it was good." The people of Singapore do nothing by half measures, so today there is the alarming possibility that there'll be no more babies.

People quickly discovered that it didn't really matter whether your child was a boy or a girl. Daughters today are professionals and retain their names after marriage so the family name lives on but sometimes the outcome may not be a happy marriage of names. The following could easily happen.

Announcement
Betty Madonna Soh
and Kelvin Elvis Low
are now the proud parents
of a baby girl
Cindy, Germaine Soh-Low

Young parent have also discovered that the fewer children they have the more time they have for each other.

And the people began to say This is Good

This is Better

This is Best.

The Singapore Tourist Promotion Board sells the concept of Instant Asia. It is this and much more because people from all over the world have come to make their homes in Singapore.

But it is Asia tourists want to see and they are seldom dis-

appointed. Tour buses whiz visitors from ultra-modern hotels and within minutes they find themselves travelling on foot down the narrow twisting lanes of Chinatown where old people who came from China sixty or seventy years ago ply their trades using methods that have not changed for a thousand years. People bargain yell at each other, walk away only to return. It can be an audio nightmare.

The night market in Chinatown is always interesting. The many tiny roadside stalls competing for space and customers sell anything from buttons to electrical gadgets. More recently the vendors, tired of shouting themselves hoarse, have come up with a novel way of attracting attention to their stalls. They have put their spiel on tape and blast it into the night. The outcome is startling but effective.

Little India, located in Serangoon Road has changed little over the years. The pungent aroma of spices assails the nostrils even before you get your first glimpse of hundreds of sarees draped in glass cabinets. The spice traders weigh, grind and mix the many ingredients that go into making those mouth-watering curries. The people are a colourful animated lot — the toss of a long shiny plait, the untying and re-tying of a dhoti, the roll of those expressive eyes and the slight shake of the head are all characteristics of the Indian race.

For those wanting to see traditional Malay shops Geyland Serai is the place to visit. Life is never static and changes are evident but the people still bargain over gold and *intan dan berlian*. Heavily embroidered material shot with gold and silver threads are still in demand. The voices here are softer, the movements less frantic because the Malays are a gentler people.

Singapore might offer insights into Asia yet it has a uniqueness all of its own.

Where else in the world can you breakfast with an *Orang Utan* named Ah Meng and people even pay for the privilege. You can be a part of a 30-trishaw convoy tearing down a busy boulevard or go back in time and enjoy your Singapore Sling under a palm tree at Raffles Hotel which has not changed much since the days of Somerset Maugham.

If there is one lasting impression visitors take away with them, it is the food. Nowhere else in the world can you find such a variety of delicious food.

Most Singaporeans are dedicated eaters. They'll unashamedly admit that most of the time they live to eat but who can blame them. Temptation is all around. Psychologists may forward theories that this is a throwback to the days when the people didn't know where their next meal was coming from. Or that with prosperity we have became degenerate guffers.

But those who know realise that eating is almost a ritual. Where to go, what to eat at what time of the year, who makes the best dish, even whom you are going to share your meal with are carefully considered. A good indication of how much you are liked could be gauged by how often you are invited for a meal.

Singapore is a dieter's hell. It is a case of food in front of you, food behind you, food to the left of you, food to the right of you and

239

when you go to a shopping centre it's food above you and even food below you.

Consider this. If we were to place every eating stall, coffee shop and restaurant side by side along the coastline of the island, they'd surely meet. It is a mind-boggling thought especially since the island has a population of only a little over 2.5 million people.

The cuisine of the world has found their way into the cooking pots of Singapore. The list goes on and on. Suffice to say that you could go through a month without repeating the fare of a single country.

But where is this place called Singapore?

A silly question? No. My colleague, Angie Chew religiously types at the bottom of all self-addressed envelopes — Singapore 1130, Republic of Singapore. She is fed-up of receiving mail locating Singapore in Hong Kong, Malaysia, Korea and even China.

One cannot really blame people for this error because even if you peer on the map of the world all you'll see is a microscopic dot. That makes us Singaporeans mere dots on a dot. A sobering thought.

The island is susceptible to change, but in itself cannot bring about change in the outside world, it can only learn to adjust to change. Despite this, people have done well for themselves. They have survived the vissitudes of time and carved for themselves and their children a niche in a land that has been acclaimed a modern miracle.

Raffles had a dream, Lee Kuan Yew and his associates made it a reality in the 21 years since Singapore became a nation state.

Gone are the slums and the racially divided transient population who only saw Singapore as the pot at the end of the rainbow, a place to accumulate wealth and then return to enjoy it in their native lands far away. They remember their roots, they are encouraged to do so but no longer wish to return to India or China.

1986 is an auspicious year for Singapore. On 9 August, it celebrated its twenty-first year as a nation. Young compared to many other nations, but what a smart, vivid, eviable youth it has grown into.